Sri Shirdi Sai Baba

The Universal Master

Sri Shirdi Sai Baba

The Universal Master

Satya Pal Ruhela

PARTRIDGE
A Penguin Random House Company

To order additional copies of this book, contact
Partridge India
000 800 10062 62
orders.india@partridgepublishing.com

www.partridgepublishing.com/india

Contents

Also by the Same Author

- *Shirdi Sai Baba – El Maestro Universal* (In Spanish)
- How Found God – *Roles played by Fakir Sai Baba and the Spirit Masters in my spiritual training resulting in God realization* [Yogi M.K.Spncer; condensed & edited by S.P.Ruhela]
- *Maine Iswar Ko Kaise Paya* [Hindi translation of the above]
- Sri Shirdi Sai Baba: The Supreme
- The Immortal Fakir of Shirdi
- Divine Grace of Sri Shirdi Sai Baba
- Sri Sathya Sai As Kalki Avatar
- Sri Sathya Sai Baba and the Future of Mankind
- *Sri Sathya Sai Baba: Leben Lehre und Werk* (In German)
- Philosophical and Sociological Foundtions of Education
- Foundation and Concept of Education
- Dimensions of Value Education
- Indian National Policy: Today and Tomorrow
- Human Values and Human Rights Education
- Joyful Learning
- Essentials of Foundations of Education
- Shirdi Sai Speaks to Yogi M.K.Spencer in Vision
- Select Spiritual Writings Writngs fof Yogi M.K.Spencer
- Unique Grace of Sri Shirdi Sai Baba
- Experiencing the Divine Grace of Sri Sathya Sai Avatar
- The Triple Incarnations of Sai Baba
- In Search of Sai Divine

Prayer

I prostrate before the *Jagatguru* (universal Mater) and
the Supreme Spirit Master Sri Shirdi Sai Baba
Who confers both temporal and spiritual blessings,
Who has an enchanting form,
Who is extremely affectionate towards His devotees
with whom He lives in the entire Universe,
Who protects righteous and uproots unrighteousness and
Who releases all creatures from bonds of *karmas*
and blesses them with eternal bliss.

Dedication

OM SAI, SRI SAI, JAI JAI SAI

This humble flower
of
my love,
shraddha(devotion)
and
Saburi (patience)
is
most reverentially offered
to
the Universal and Ascended Master Sri Shirdi Sai Baba
on
His 97th Birth Anniversary
On
the 27th September, 1838

Preface

Sri Shirdi Sai Baba (1838-1918) is universally worshipped as a very great spiritual personality. He was the incarnation of Lord Shiva and Lord Dattatrya and reincarnation of the medieval saint poet Kabir. He was the first Sai Baba in the Trinity of Sai Baba incarnations – the second one was Sri Sathya Sai Baba (1926-2011) and the third one - future Prema Sai Baba- is expected to come in this very 21st century.

Sri Shirdi Sai Baba lived the life of a simple, poor, illiterate *Fakir* in Shirdi (Maharastra State) in an old dilapidated mosque which He named 'Dwarkamai'. His name and fame as a kind, benevolent saint, miraculously helping all those who remember Him, have been spreading like wild fire throughout the world during the last five decades. His devotes are living throughout the world. His temples are in India and many foreign countries like USA,UK., Germany, Mauritius, African and eastern countries, Japan, China etc.and even in remote islands. The Pacific island of Niue has recemntly on *Guru Purnima* festival day (31st July,2015) issued gold coins of Sai Baba image of 2 and 4 gms. All these facts show His worldwide following.

It was my good fortune to have been mysteriously drawn under His divine grace and that of the second Sai Baba –Sri Sathya Sai Baba of Puttarparthi (Andhra Pradesh) in 1974. I developed great faith in and deep feeelngs of love and dedication for Him, visited His holy township of Shirdi many times and collected all published information. Being a social science researcher I searched out a number of pieces of new information on Him and then wrote this book and many other books on Him and also some books on Sri Sathya Sai Baba. My books have been appreciated by Sai devotees and thus I have received the blessings of both the Sai *avatars* and the good will of spiritual seekers all over the world.

The idea of writing this book projecting Sai Baba as the Universal Master was given by Sri H.D.Lakshman Swami Ji of Bangalore and then the blessings of Sri Shirdi Sai Baba and His great devotees Shivamma They, Sri Shivesh Swami ji of Shirdi and the then Executive Officer and Public Relations Officer of Sri Sai Baba *Sansthan* (Trust) were obtained by me and Lakshman Swami Ji on 13th August, 1992.

I am happy to recall how this book was conceived was when I most unexpectedly met him for the first time. We met in the second class compartment of K.K.Express train in which I was travelling from New Delhi to reach Sri Sathya Sai Baba's Prasanthi Nilayam *ashram*. Sri Lakhman Swami He was returning to his place Bangalore from his pilgrimage to Shirdi. After silently watching me for some time he suddenly got Sai Baba's message in his intuition and conveyed to me: "Brother, although we have never met earlier and I do not know about you yet while silently watching you for some time just now I have got the divine intuition that you are" *Bhagwati Swaroop* (the very form of Saraswati, the Goddess of Learning). You are now thinking of writing a ook on Sri Shirdi Sai Baba. You should highlight Sri Shirdi Sai Baba's unique status and role as the "Universal Master' which aspect has so far not been projected by most of the writers on Sai Baba. *Sadguru* Shirdi Sai Baba wishes so, and this is His divine assignment for you. Would you accept it with pleasure?" I readily accepted it and told him that I was going to Sathya Sai Baba's place Putttaparthi for his *darshan* and would return to New Delhi after a week. Then he told me "Please meet me at my house-cum-temple of Banashankari Devi (Goddess Parvati - the Consort of Lord Shiva) in Bangalore. He gave me his address saying: "When you will be coming to Bangalore from Puttaparthi after a few days on your return journey to New Delhi in order to take the K.K.Expresss from Bangalore Junction, please come to my place and stay with me for the night. I shall then perform special worship of Goddess Banashankari Devi, Consort of Lord Shiva, for obtaining her blessings on you for the successful completion of this new project of writing this book. Then you return to your place and there you should prepare the tentative Table of Contents of the proposed book and then bring it to Shirdi on the mutually agreed day in the next month to seek the blessings of Sri Shirdi Sai Baba. I would reach there and we both shall pray at the Sai Baba's *Gurushthan* and *Samadhi Mandir* to seek Sai Baba's divine blessings on your book project."

Accordingly, after a week I came to Bangalore and reached my place in the evening of 24th July 1992. After the late evening *bhajans* and departure of the *mandali* (group) of his devotees I performed the special worship of the

Goddess seeking her blessings and gave me her *prashad* and some *dakshina* (cash gift) and her blessings. Thereafter, in the next month we met at Shirdi on the auspicious day of 13ᵗʰ August 1992 and prayed to Sai Baba for His blessings and also met the eminent Sai devotee (Late) Sri Shivnesh Swami Ji, Executive Officer and Public Relations Officer gave their best wishes for this project. Then I wrote this book with great interest and dedication in spite of many difficulties, lack of funds and other severe problems in early 1990s which was a difficult phase of my ljfe. Sai Baba's grace then steered my boat and I could complete this book with the cooperation of the Public Relations Officer of Sri Sai Baba *Sansthan* (Trust).They all blessed me profusely for the completion of this book project.

Later on I learnt that Sri Lakshmanm Swami ji, born on 4.12.1938 at Honnalli village, Tiptur Taluka, Karnataka State, was a great spiritualist and social worker of Bangalre, He was said to be the reincarnation of Maharishi Agustya and blessed with a number of spiritual attainments and born with the power to reveal past *karmas* and future happenings, cure and bless people. Till 1993 He had established 30 Seva centers and temples and was the great devotee oflord Shiva.ans His consort Banashankari Devi. Adi Shankaracharya and Sri Shirdi Sai Baba. He was a great devotee of Sri Shivamma Thayee- then 102 years old only surviving contempory devotee of Sri Shirdi Sai Baba, it was due to hs motivatioin and helpthat I was oprivilged to interview her on 25.7.1992 and seeekher blessings and and write the book '*My LifeWith Sri Shirdi Sai Baba-Thrilling Memories of Shivamma Thayee,102 years old, the only surviving devoee of Shirdi Sai Baba*' (1992).

The readers may thus appreciate that this book was the result of the sole divine wish, inspiration, mysterious grace and help of Sri Sai Baba. I am very happy to recall and record this background story of this great book now for the first time for the information of all.

This book t was first published by Sterling Publishers in 1994 and they reprinted it in 1995, 1996 and 1998. In 2007 I changed the publisher and gave to Diamond Pocket Books Pvt. Ltd. Co., which was publishing my many other books. I have had very unfortunate experience of being exploitedby this second publishing company. The Diamond Pocket Books did not pay my due royalties on this book (like my other many books) although they had made agreements with me to pay only 5% royalty. They have been bringing out many new editions and innumerable secret reprints of it and my other books. Most of my books in English were ISBN marked, they were advertized and sold by prominent international web-sites of booksellers.

The readers will be shocked to know the following most stunning bare facts about this book *'Sri Shirdi Sai Baba: The Universal Master'* which was first published by Diamond Pocket in 2007 and republished.

SRI SHIRDI SAI BABA: THE UNIVERSAL MASTER International Standard Book No. 81-288-1517-2 First Edition was published in <u>Feb.,2007:</u> Price Rs.95/-

Further Reprints and Editions: Announced as <u>NEW PUBLICATION</u> in their own publicity monthly *'Diamond Pusk Samachar'* of:

- April (ii)2007
- June(I) 2007
- Sept,2009
- **May(I),2010 (enhanced price Rs.100/-**
- July, 2010) *as discovered from the web site: websstores.com/search.all.*
- *com(p.4):pub.date.Mon.08Aug 2007*

But Royalty (@5%) was paid to me on **500 books only**-Rs.2,750/-(Half of Rs.4,750/ -vide cheque No. 685181 dt.7.10.2008 drawn on ICICI Bank This was most unjust and unfair – it was just a pittance, as thousands of copies were published in the first Edition in Feb.2008 and thousands of copies in each of the reprints in that year FY 2007-08.

No royalty has been paid on this book thereafter since 2008 till this date in 2015 even though lakhs of copies of this book have been printed in many further New Editions and countless reprints of each of the First Edition and each of the further New Editions during the last seven. (2007-8 – 2014-15)

1. 1ˢᵗ Edition was published in Feb.2007: As announced in *Diamond Pustak Samachar'*, Feb. 2007

2. Further Editions Reprints: Announced as <u>NEW PUBLICATION</u> in *Diamond Pusk Samachar* of:

- April (i) 2007
- April (ii)2007
- June(I) 2007
- Sept,2009
- May(I),2010 (enhanced price Rs.100/-
- July (2010)
- Discovered from *alwebsstores.com/search.all.com(p.4):* <u>pub.date. Mon.08Aug 2007</u>

In spite of their publishing these numerous reprints/new editions and many other unknown no. of reprints and selling thousands of copies of this book in the world in the F.Y. 2007-08, the publisher Diamond Pocket Books paid after much harassment and delay most unjustly paid me royalty on merely 500 copies of this book, i.e. Rs <u>2375/--</u>only – half the amount of Rs.4,750<u>/- of Cheque No.6851851 Dt.7.1.2009 which amount was for only 500 copies each of his two books *(Sri Shirdi Sai Baba: The Universal Master* (Rs.95/-) and *"Sri Shirdi Sai Baba ke Divya Chamatkar"* of</u> which unknown no. of copies had been printed by them during FY 2007 -08.

3. <u>Further Edition or Reprint in 2009: *Mlbd.com*</u>

4. <u>Further NEW Publication/ Edition PROOF;</u> *Diamond Pustak Samachar,* (30 March 2012 New edition. Price enhanced to Rs.100/-

PROOF: www.*mlbd.com. The* Photo copy of the web@*mlbd.com* advertisement of this book & nine other books on Sai Baba by meshowing the enhanced price Rs. 100/- of as many as 7 out of 8 books as notified in the web advertisement.

I have discovered that the following web site of international book sellers have advertised and sold this book:

1. <u>ttp://www.alwebsstores.com/search.all.com(p4)pub, date.Mon.08Aug.</u> 2007.
2. http:/www.mlbd.com in 2009
3. <u>http://ww,mlbd,com</u> in 2012 & 2013
4. http:ww:crossword.in

5. http://ebay.in/htm
6. http://www.yasni.com/ruhela.check+people/sai%2obaba
7. http://www.WebWay,in,htm/Sri-Shirdi-SaI-Baba-Universal-Master –Prof Satya Pal-Ruhela
8. deastores
9. OmpllBooks,
   - In 2010, the publisher advertised in their bi-lingual publicity journal*'Diamond Pustak Samachar',* March

(First)2010, page 9 that this book *'Sri Shirdi Sai Baba: The Universal Master"* as one of their publishing company's <u>"100 BEST SELLER"</u> books..

What does a "BEST SELLER' of the renowned international publisher Diamond Pocket Books Pvt. Ltd. imply? This is the most crucial question.

DIAMOND POCKET BOOKS PRESENTS:
BEST SELLER OF 2010
100 DAYS 10 LAKH COPIES
RELEASE IN 100 CITIES
"The 4th Idiot"

This clearly shows that the criteria of "100 SELLER" category book of Diamond Pocket Books is that its 10 Lakh copies were/are sold in a year.

CLAIM:

(A) Therefore, it is logical for me to believe that this famous ISBN marked book 'Sri Shirdi Sai Baba: The Universal Master', which oo was announced as one of the 100 BEST SELLERS in two issues of *Diamond Books Samachar* of 15-30 Jan. 2010 on page 15, andof 1-15 March, 2010, also must have been sold in ten lakh copies –if not in 100 days in 2009 in India but certainly in 36 months or three years period from February.2007 to February 2010 during which period many reprints/editions have been secretly printed without ever informing me, the author who is the copy right owner, and sold throughout world. It has been discovered from the Internet searches that many websites of international book sellers as mentioned above have been advertising and selling this best seller internationally known spiritual book on Sri Shirdi Sai Baba who continues to be venerated by millions of devotees and spiritual seekers throughout the world. Therefore, the publisher is liable to pay the royalty on 10 lakh copies sold during the three period from FY. 2007-08 to FY.2010,i.e,: <u>10,00000 copies sold @ 5% Royalty on Rs.95/ - the Selling price of the book = 1,00000 x Rs. 4.75each book = Rs.47,50,000/-</u>minus Rs,2,375/- only which had been paid on just 500 copies only forthe FY 2007-08 (vide Cheque for Rs.4,750/- dt.7.10.2009 referred to above. = <u>Rs.47,49835/</u>-(A)

(B) <u>FURTHER CLAIM:</u> Further New Editions have been published in 2010 and on 30 March 2012 and many reprints thereof have been published and sold during 2013-14, with enhanced Selling Price of Rs.100/- w.e.f. March, 2012 (actually from 2009) PROOFS; (V) Further NEW Publication/Edition. PROOF; *Diamond Pustak Samachar,* (30 March 2012 NEW Edition Price enhanced to Rs.100/-It is modestly assumed that on a average at least one lakh copies of this book during each of the Financial Years 20010-11, 20011-12 & 2012 -13 and 20913-15 might have been sold, the Diamond Pocket Books is liable to pay me as its author.

It has been found out that this and my some other books have contemned to be sold on line by *web@mlbd,com* (of Motilal Banarasi Das Co.,New Delhi). They have been advertising and selling book for Rs.100/-since 2000-10

This is not only in case of this book. The same sort of gross unfairness, high handedness and exploitation of me as author has been done by the Diamond Pocket Books publisher in case of all my other pocket books.

After being thus cheated and severely exploited by the dishonest publisher for so long, I ultimately decided to fight out against the grave injustice of the publisher. Despite my old age and my being surrounded by so many health, financial, social problems and lack of material help and even moral support from anybody, but having total faith in the identical great teachings of Lord Krishna and Sri Sai Baba I mustered courage and decided to challenge the dishonest powerful publishing co. legally. I filed a case of royalty dispute against the Co. in the High Court of Delhi in 2012. The High Court in August 2013 appointed a Sole Arbitrator to settle this royalty dispute. I then filed my claim petition with all concrete proofs with the Sole Arbitrator in May 2014.The arbitration proceedings are now going on and the judgment will be known in near future.

My experiences with some other Indian publishers also have been unhappy. I had such sad experience with the dishonest publishers of India who came in my life, they only exploited me by not paying the due royalties on my very important and popular spiritual books in Hindi for long.

When I was so disappointed, I providentially, mysteriously and unexpectedly received a phone call from Mr.Nelson Cortez, Senior Publishing Consultant of the renowned American publishing Co. - Partridge India of the world renowned Partridge Random Penguin group of internationally reputed publishing companies. He was very courteous and encouraging and he assured me that his publishing Co. would like to publish my books under any of their self-publishing packages. I prayed to Sai Baba for His direction. and as guided by Him in 2013 I approached Mr.Nelson Cortez with my book proposals three in 2013 and two in early 2014. They have by now published my four books and the fifth one is expected soon by the end of 2015.

In July 2515, Mr.Franco Martinz of the same publishing Co. enquired of me if I had still more books and was thinking to get them published by Partridge India publishing Co. I wanted to publish my two most important and well known books-this one and *Divine Grace of Sri Shirdi Sai Baba* and so I agreed to give them also to Partridge INhe India Co.. Thus they are now publishing the revised and updated edition of this book *Sri Shirdi Sai Baba: The Universal Master*.The second book will come after this. All these books are under their Amethyst Self-publishing package. They will be available in both paperback and e mail formats throughout the world.

May Sri Shirdi Sai Baba shower His grace on all the readers as He been kind to me. My life has been saved many times by His grace and I have been able to continue pursuing my spiritual writing work even at this advanced age of 80. Although I cannot walk, stand, travel and speak legibly and do any physical activity and have been greatly suffering from economic, health and many problems yet I am able to work on my personal computer for some time daily and maintain poise and peace by following Sri Sai Baba's two commands – *shraddha* (devotion) and *saburi* (patience, contentment). This is the concrete evidence of Sai Baba's grace and mercy on me

S.P.Ruhela
spruhela@gmail,com

Acknowledgements

I gratefully acknowledge the following for their kindness, inspiration, good will and help:

- SrI Shirdi Sai Baba
- (Late) Sri Shivnesh Swami, Shirdi
- Sri H.D.Lakshman Swami Bangalore
- (Late)i Shivamma Thayee, Bangalore
- (Late) Sri B.Uma Maheswara Rao
- (Late) Sri A.Somasundaram, Markapur
- Sri T.R.Naidu,Hyderabad
- (Late) Sri J.M.Chinoy,Nagpur
- ((Late) Sri T.R.Ramnathen,Sarangpur
- (Late) Sri M.R.Raghunathan,Chennai
- Sri Seethmma 'Baba Patti'
- Dr.Karunakaran Jyothida,Chennai
- Sri Radha Krisna *Sai Jeevi*',Bangalore
- Sri Chakor Ajgaonkar,Thane
- Sri V.B.Kher,Mumbai
- Justice Rajendra Saksena, Jaipur
- Sri K.C.Bakiwala,Jaipur
- Mr.Nelson Cortez, Senior Publishing Consultant, Partridge India
- Mr. Franco Martinez, Supervisor, Patridge India
- Mr.Pohar Baruah, Publishing Services Associate, Patridge India, and many other Sai devotees, authors, friends and well-wishers

- S.P.Ruhela

Chapter - 1
Sri Shirdi Sai Baba: A Brief Profile

"I am parvardigar (God). I live at Shirdi and everywhere. My age is lakhs of years.My business is to give blessings. All things are Mine. I give everything to everyone."

-Sri Shirdi Sai Baba

Sri Sai Baba of Shirdi was born on Thursday, the 27th September 1838, in the forest near Pathri village in Aurangabad district of Maharashtra. His parents were high-caste Brahmins of the Bharadwaja *gotra*. His father's name was Ganga Bavadia. His parents and grandparents worshipped their family deity Hanuman of Kumhar *bavadi* (water tank), on the outskirts of Pathri village. Since they lived near the *bavadi*, they were known as *Bavadia* (one who owns or lives near a *bavadi*). Baba's parental house (No. 4-438-61) situated in Vaishnav *Gali* (street) has many years back been bought by the local people, who formed *"Shri Sai Smarak Mandir Samiti"* and erected a shed where local Sai devotees have been performing arti (worship) of Sai Baba every Thursday.

Sai Baba's father, Ganga Bavadia, was a poor boatman of Pathri. His mother was Devagiriamma. The religious parents not only worshipped Hanuman but also Lord Shiva and Shakti. They did not have a child for many years after marriage. Suddenly, one night Lord Shiva and His consent Shakti came to their house when Devagiriamma was alone, her husband having gone to the riverside to save his boat from the rainy and stormy night. The divinity blessed Devagiriamma with three children and assured that Lord Shiva Himself would be born as her third child. As a result of this divine blessing, one son and one daughter were born to Devagiriamma. While the third was yet to be born, her

1

husband developed *vairagya* (detachment) and decided to forsake his family and go away to the forest to worship God.

Devagiriamma also decided to follow her husband. She sent her two children to her mother's house and accompanied him to the forest. The couple had hardly gone a few miles when birth pangs set in. She implored her husband to wait for a while, but he kept on going his way. Devagiriamma delivered the child all alone in the forest under a banyan tree, placed the newborn, covering it with leaves, on the ground and leaving it there, hastened after her husband. Sri Sai Baba so told His devotees about His mother:

"My mother was greatly rejoicing that she had got a son (i.e., Me). I was, for My part, wondering at her conduct. When did she beget Me? Was I begotten at all? Have I not been already in existence? Why is she rejoicing as such?"

Hardly had a few minutes passed when an elderly Muslim *faqir* named Patil, returning with his wife from His in-law's place in a *tonga* (horse cart), reached the very spot where the newborn child was lying covered in leaves. The *fakir's* wife *fakiri* alighted from the tonga to ease herself. She was surprised to hear the soft cries of a newborn babe. Excited by such a revelation she called her husband to the spot and showed him the baby. As they were childless, they at once thought that *Allah* (God) had sent that baby for them; they took the child with them to their house in Manwat village and brought it up as their own son, and named him 'Babu'. The *fakir* died after four years. After her husband's death *fakiri* was at the tether's end, as the child 'Babu', was always doing strange and abnormal acts offensive to her religion. He would go the Hindu shrines and recite the *Quran*, or install a stone *Shivalinga* in a mosque and worship it or play marbles and win a *Saligram* from the moneylender's son, or sing songs in praise of *Allah* in Hindu temples and say "Rama is God, Shiva is *Allah*" and so on. Puzzled at such behaviour and with scores of daily complaints from Hindus and Muslims against Babu, *faqiri* eventually decided to carry Babu to Sailu and entrust him to the charge of a pious and spiritually elevated Brahmin, Guru Venkusha, who was running an ashram for the orphaned, abandoned and poor boys of all communities. Actually, Venkusha's real name was Gopala Rao Deshmukh. In one of his earlier births, he had been the famous Hindu *Guru* Ramananda of the medieval saint Kabir at Banaras while Shirdi Sai Baba Himself had been his disciple Kabir at the time.

Babu stayed at Guru Venkusha's *ashram* for about 12 years, i.e., from 1842 to 1854. He was much loved by his Guru because of His staunch devotion.

Sai Baba told one of His devotees, Radha Bai Deshmukh, about His Guru Venkusha in these moving words:

"...I had a *Guru*. He was a great Saint and most merciful. I served him long, very long; still he would not blow any *mantra* into my ears. I had keen desire, never to leave him, but to stay, serve him at all costs and receive some instructions from him.

I resorted to my *Guru* for 12 years. He brought me up. There was no dearth of food and clothing. He was full of love, nay he was the love incarnate. How can I describe him? When I looked at him he seemed as if he was in deep meditation and then both of us were filled with bliss. Night and day, I gazed at him with no thought of hunger and thirst. Without him, I felt restless. I had no other object to meditate on, nor any other thing than my *Guru* to attend to.He never neglected me, but protected me at all times. I lived with him and was sometimes away from him, still I never felt the want or absence of his love..."

Because of Guru Venkusha's great love for Babu, other boys of the *ashram* grew jealous of him. Once when Babu had been sent by Venkusha to fetch *bilva* leaves from the forest for worship, a group of boys overpowered him here; they beat him up and one boy even hit him on His forehead with a brick, which started bleeding profusely. The other boys fled away from the scene. He took the brick with him and came to *Guru* Venkusha who was deeply grieved to see Babu in that miserable condition. He tore a *dhoti* (loin cloth) and bandaged the wound on His forehead. He shed tears to see the brick, which had hit Babu's head. Thereafter, Venkusha advised Babu to leave his *ashram* with warm blessings, unlimited divine powers and directions. He gave him the parting gifts of the brick and a piece of cloth and directed him to go towards the Godavari river.

Thus, the next evening (in 1854 Babu left *Guru* Venkusha's *ashram* all alone taking the brick with him, and within a few days reached Shirdi on foot. An old woman of Shirdi, the mother on one Nana Chopdar, who saw this 16 years old ascetic, left behind this description:

"This young lad, fair, smart and very handsome, was first seen under the *neem* (margosa) tree, seated in an *asana* (yogic posture). The people of the village were wonderstruck to see such a young lad practicing hard penance, not minding heat and cold. By day he associated with none, by night he was afraid of none...outwardly he looked very young but by his actions he was really a great soul. He was the embodiment of dispassion and was an enigma to all..."

He stayed at Shirdi barely for two months and one day suddenly left the place. He wandered from place to place for a few years without disclosing his identity to anyone. Most of his followers and devotees till today do not know any details of his activities during those unknown years. Decades later Sai Baba, however, once told his close devotees:

"When I was a youngster, in search of bread and butter, I went to Badaum. There I got an embroidery work. I worked hard, sparing no paint! The employer was very much pleased with me. Three other boys worked before me. The first got Rs.50/-, the second Rs.100/-, and the third Rs.150/- while I was given twice the whole of this amount. Seeing my cleverness, the employer presented me a full dress, a turban for the head and a shawl for the body, etc. I kept this dress intact without using it. I thought that what a man might give does not last long and is imperfect but what my *Sircar* (Lord or God) gives, lasts to the end of time."

In a forest near the twin villages Sindhon-Bindhon, 24 Kms south of Aurangabad, a rich Muslim, Chand Patil, resident of Dhoop Kheda village, met the young *faqir* (Babu) who did the fascinating miracle of calling Patil's lost mare 'Bijli' and materializing live charcoals and water by thrusting a pair of tongs into the earth. Chand Patil invited the young *faqir* (Babu was then dressed like a Muslim *fakir*) to his village Dhoop Kheda. At Dhoop Kheda, He performed a number of thrilling miracles.

After some days, He accompanied Chand Patil's party to Shirdi in bullock carts, where the marriage of Patil's nephew was to take place.While the marriage party moved to the bride's house, he young faqir went to the Khandoba temple near the road. Mlahaspati, the priest of Khandoba temple in Shirdi, welcomed the return of the *faqir* after four years and spontaneously addressed him by uttering words *"Ya, Sai"* (Come, Sai), and since that memorable day that *faqir* came to be known as Sai Baba of Shirdi. He made Shirdi His permanent abode and physically never went out beyond a radius of five miles. He achieved the *nirvana* (the cessation of individual existence) on Tuesday, the 15th of October 1918 on the Dushera festival day. He thus lived for 80 yearstlllo 1918,

It was during his permanent stay at Shirdi from 1858 to 1918 that he performed all his thrilling *leelas* (divine sports), miracles, spiritual transformation and granted *mukti* (liberation) to innumerable creatures – human beings, animals, insect, etc. all drawn to him as if by magic. He lived like a Sufi *fakir* in an old deserted mosque, which he named as *"Dwarka*

The deception did not work for long because the villagers of Shirid and His devotees from all over Maharashtra and South Indian states soon succeeded in finding out his reality as an *avatar* (incarnation) of a very high order, Rarely did he declare publicly that he himself was God; most of the time he behaved as if he was merely a servant of God: *"Allah malik hai"* (God alone is the Lord and Master). But he once demonstrated that He was the incarnation of Lord Dattatreya – the three headed son of Sage Atri and his wife Anasuya, a combined incarnation of the Trinity-Brahma, Vishnu and Shiva. He also revealed that he had been Saint Kabir of the 14th-15th centuries in one of his previous births. To many of his devotees, he demonstrated that he was in fact, *Sarva-devtaswaroopam* (all gods and goddesses rolled into one). He demonstrated through His breathtaking miracles how He was present in all the forms of gods and goddesses and saints of all faiths

A Sai devotee unknwn to me (Late) M.R. Raghunathan of Chennai had in July 1995 sent me the horoscope of Sri Shirdi Sai Baba discovered from *Sri Agustya nad*i with the *nadi* astrologer Dr.A.Karunakaran, in which it was mentioned that Sri Shirdi Sai Baba was born on Thrsday, the 27th Sept., 1838(Tamil year *Vilambhi, Vikrama* year 1895, *Hijri* 1254 (*J. Akhir*), Month—Tamil *Purattasi, Kanya*; 13th (Tamil Date in month *Kanya, Rasi Shukra, Lagna Raviu*. His parents were Sri Ganga Bhavadia (Brahmin) and Smt. Devagiriamma. Mother Smt. Devagiriamma was reborn as Smt. R. Seethamal of Chenai, Sai Baba's elder brother Ambadass was reborn as. R.Raghunathan, and Sai Baba's elder sister Smt. Balwant Bai was reborn as Mrs. P.Rajeshwari, daughter of Seethammal who was known as 'Baba Paati.'. I travelled to Chennai and interviewed all those persons and published a small book *'Sri Shirdi Sai Baba's Mother's Reincarnation'* in 1995.

A keen researcher on the Baba, B.V. Kher had discovererd by his field research in the 1970s that Sri Shirdi Sai Baba most probably belonged tothe Bhusari family of the Brahmins of Pathri village and his parental house(No. 4-438-61)

5

was situated in Vaishnav Gali. That house was later onbought by B.V. Kher and donated to the local people who formed *"Shri SaiSmarak Mandir Samiti"*. This *Samiti* has erected a shed and temple for localSai Devotees to perform *aart*i (worship) of Sri Shirdi Sai Baba..

The name of SriShirdi Sai Baba is knowm all over theworld. The spiritual saga of Sai Baba of Shirdi is today fast spreading to all the corners of the world. Shirdi Sai Baba temples have been established in most of the Indian townships and across the oceans, in metropolises like London (UK), Los Angeles (USA), Loredo (USA), Canberra (Australia), Durban (South Africa), Lagos (Nigeria) etc. Today, among his large number of devotees are Germans, Austrians, Africans, New Zealanders, who are all enamored with his unlimited wealth of spirituality and simple personality.

It is indeed a most thrilling and challenging mystery for all spiritual seekers, intellectuals and Sai devotees of all faiths and countries to unravel, understand and appreciate how living and working within the traditional rural social context of Shirdi of the late 18th and early 19th centuries, the humble Sai Baba *fakir* of *Dwarka Mai Masjid*, emerged as the most powerful and influential spiritual Messiah, the great Universal Master for the entire humanity, who inaugurated an era of spiritual awakening in the world.

We may recall that Shirdi Sai Baba's sojourn on the earth from 1838 to 1918 was during the most difficult and thorny period of the history of human civilization. Industrial revolution had proliferated exploitation by the colonial powers of the underdeveloped countries throughout the world. The First World War was fought and there was unmitigating misery and violence spreading far and wide. In India, the British rulers, the *Rajas, Nawabs, Jagirdars* and their puppets and instruments of exploitation were sucking the blood of their subjects. The first battle of India's independence in 1857 was fought by patriots like Rani Lakshmi Bai of Jhansi, Nana Phadnavis, Bahadur Shah Zafar of Delhi, etc., but the Indians had been defeated in this attempt: the Indian National Congress had taken birth and the Indian patriots had gain started their struggle to achieve *Swaraj* (Independence). The dominant features of the contemporary Indian society were ritualism, communal tensions among the Hindus and Muslims, casteism, untouchability, racial segregation, poverty and an overall specter of gloom.

It is really a wonderful story as to how, without the backing of any powerful religious or political organization or the support of any patron, or any specific religious idiosyncrasy or a cult of fanatic zealots and, in the absence of any paraphernalia or great fanfare of guruhood and publicity, Sri Sai Baba of Shirdi, living in the most humble, simple and traditional rural background, single-handedly sowed the seeds of communal amity and harmony. All this was achieved by the basic principles of *atmic* unity, oneness of soul, spiritualization and attainment of peace and human dignity by respecting man, regardless of his race, nation or creed in the strifeful society. What he taught through his parables and stories, as also through his brief observations and teachings to his devotees, was the most refined common quintessential spiritual religious tradition of all the faiths of mankind presented in a very simple, direct and penetrating words which enlivened every heart.

Who was this Sai Baba of Shirdi in reality? Some say that he was an *avadhoota*, some an *auliya*, some a con man; while some opine him to be a great and unique saint of the era.

Sri Mehar Baba, who himself was an important *avatar* and a disciple of Shirdi Sai Baba's most blessed disciple, Sri Upasani Maharaj, said this about Sri Sai Baba:

"You will never be able to understand thoroughly how great Sai Baba was! He was the personification of perfection. If you know Him as I know Him you will call Him the Master of creation."

Sri Sathya Sai Baba of Puttaparthi (Andhra Pradesh) revealed this about Sri Shirdi Sai Baba:

"Shirdi Sai Baba was a *Brahma-Jnani*. He was the embodiment of Universal Consciousness – *Jnaneswaroopa*. He was also the *Sadguru*, teaching His devotees the reality, and guiding them along the path of Truth. He was a *Poornavatar* (full or integral incarnation) and possessed all the attributes of a Poornavatar. He had all the attributes of divine *Shakti* (power) but held them in check and did not reveal them fully. He was like a learned musician who exhibited his musical skill occasionally; He was like a gifted poet who gave voice to his verse only rarely; He was like a skilled sculptor who revealed his artistry only sometimes....*siddhis* (miracles) and *leelas* (sports) were merely outpourings of (His) love for His devotees. They were not meant to attract but only to safeguard and protect. He did not use them like visiting-cards. He used His *Shakti* only to save His ardent devotees from distress and trouble, from sorrow and pain. His advent was for revealing the essence of true divinity."

To describe such a great divine personality or Prophet is not only a gigantic task but at the same time very thrilling and fortunate task. It is on record that when Sri Shirdi Sai Baba's ardent devotee, Anna Saheb Dabolkar, sought Baba's permission to write the first book on His divine life and *leelas*, Baba blessed him with these words to Shama, who had pleaded for Hemadpant's request:

"Let him make a collection of stories and experiences, keep notes and memos; I will help him. He is only an outward instrument. I myself would write My life and satisfy the wishes of My devotees. He should get rid of his ego, place it at My feet. He who acts thus in life, him I help most.

...Hearing My stories and teachings will create faith in devotees hearts and they will easily get self-realization and bliss; let there be no insistence on establishing one's own view, no attempt to refute others, opinions, no discussion of pros and cons of any subject.

...If My *leelas* are written, the *avidhya* (nescience) will vanish and if they are attentively and devotedly listened to, the consciousness of the worldly existence will abate giving place to strong waves of devotion and love and if one dives deep into My *leelas*, he would get precious jewels of knowledge."

I earnestly believe that these words blessings, guidance and assurance of Sri Shirdi Sai Baba, a great increnation of God, were not for Hemadpant alone who was the author of *Sri Sai Charita*, the first biography of Baba, but also for all the future writers of biographies and books on Him, His devotees, worshippers of His grace for all times to come. This great assurance of Sri Shirdi Sai Baba has, in fact, been the motivation for the author to write this book on Him.

Spiritual Heredity

Sri Shirdi Sai Baba was not an ordinary saint. He was God descended in Human form in 1838. He had revealed that His age was 'lakhs of years". He taken innumerable births and had lived in many generations with a number of people who were His contemporaries in Shirdi.

There are five widely prevalent beliefs about the spiritual heredity of Shirdi Sai Baba:

1. He was the full incarnation of Lord Shiva.
2. He was the third incarnation of Lord Dattatreya – the Trinity of Brahma, the Creator; Vishnu the Sustainer, and Shiva, the Destroyer.

The first two notable incarnations of Dattatreya wer Sri Sripada Srivallabh and Sri Narsimha Saraswati, of the 14th and 15th centuries.

3. He was reat *yogis*, which was started, by Lord Shiva, *Guru* Machindernath and *Guru* Gorakhnath.

4. He was in the incarnation of Kabir, the great iconoclastic saint of medieval India who laid stress on spirituality without ritualism and preached communal harmony among all people.

5. As incarnation of Lord Shiva

Sri Sathya Sai Baba of Puttaparthi (Andhra Pradesh), who claimed himself to be the combined contemporary incarnation of Lord Shiva and Shakti (the consort of Shiva) and also the incarnation of Shirdi Sai Baba, narrated the following story publicly in 1986:

"Thousands of years ago, the great sage Bharadwaja, wishing to master all the Vedas, was advised by Indra (the ruler of Gods) to perform a *yagya* (Vedic ritual). Eager to have Shakti preside over it and receive Her blessing, Bharadwaja left for Kailash (a sacred peak in the Himalayas), the abode of Shiva and Shakti, to convey the invitation. Finding them entranced in the cosmic dance, Bharadwaja waited for eight days – apparently ignored by them, and obviously failing to comprehend the welcoming smile cast on him by *Shakti*.

Unhappy and disappointed, Bharadwaja decided to return home, fell in a stroke and his left side was paralyzed as a result of cold and fatigue. Shiva then approached and cured him completely by sprinkling on him water from the *Kamandalu* (vessel). Consoled by Shiva, Bharadwaja, was granted boons by both Shiva and *Shakti*, who were also pleased to attend the *yagya*. Shiva promised the *Rishi* (sage) that they would both take human form and be born thrice in the Bharadwaja *gotra* (lineage) – Shiva alone at Shirdi as Sai Baba; Shiva and Shakti together at Puttaparthi as Sathya Sai Baba; and then Shakti alone as Prema Sai...(Rishi Bhardwaja had received this boon about 5600 years ago).

As Incarnation of Lord Dattatreya

In his *Sri Guru Charita*, Acharya E. Bhardwaja recalled a saint Sri Gulavani Maharaja, a direct disciple of Sri Vasudevananda Saraswati, telling him, "He (Shirdi Sai Baba) is the *avatar* of Lord Dattatreya. He manifests Himself to His worthy devotees even today in His physical form and guides them."

9

The story of Lord Dattatreya is that Anasuya, wife of the great sage *Atri*, became famous for her *(pativratya)*. devotion to her husband Such was her spiritual power that even the hard and uneven earth turned soft and smooth for her as she walked over it. Even the scorching sun and blazing fire turned cool in regard to her. The god of wind did not dare to blow except as a pleasant breeze for her sake. The gods presiding over nature's forces were afraid that they would lose their dignity if they defied her greatness and so sought refuge from Lord Vishnu, the sustainer of all existence.

Once Sage Narada, who freely moves in the three words, visited the abodes of Brahma, Vishnu and Shiva and proclaimed the spiritual eminence of Anasuya which was a result of her intense and unrivalled devotion to her husband and of her unfaltering vow of hospitality to visitors. Hearing this, the consorts of the divine Trinity, i.e. Saraswati, Lakshmi and Parvati, felt jealous of her and wept. When their husbands tried to console them, they insisted that they should find an occasion to curse Anasuya Devi, or trap her in moral dilemma and see that her greatness did not exceed theirs. So the three gods went to the hermitage of Sage *Atri*, disguised as three unexpected and unknown guests *(atithis)*. Anasuya welcomed the guests with due respect and seated them. As per her vow of dutifulness, she said, "Holy Sirs, you have sanctified our hermitage by your holy visit. I heartily welcome you. Please say what I can do for you. The master of the hermitage, sage *Atri*, has gone to the forest to perform his austerities *(tapas)*." The guests told her that they were all very hungry and could not wait till her husband returned. They wanted to eat immediately. She went in and after making proper arrangements invited them to lunch. Then the guests said, "Holy one! Unless you take off your clothes and serve us food in your nakedness, we shall not eat but go away hungry!" On hearing their words, she smiled to herself and reflected thus: "I am totally purified by the long association with Sage *Atri*. What harm can the god of lust ever do to me? So I need fear nothing. If I do not comply with their precondition, they would go away cursing me for failure in my duty and my promise to feed them. As they have sought food from my hands, I look upon them as my own children and not as strangers or grown-up men."

Having decided thus, she said to them, "Sirs, I shall do as you wish, come and have your lunch!" Then as she unrobed herself, by virtue of her superior spiritual power, the divine guests were at once transformed into infants. At the sight of them, holy and motherly love swelled up in her heart to intensely that her bosom experienced lactation. She happily suckled them and the three infants were immensely satisfied. Brahma, Vishnu and Shiva, as though exhausted with their tasks of creation, sustenance and destruction had all enjoyed perfect bliss in her lap.

Then Anasuya realized that they were the Holy Trinity and was very happy. She put them in a cradle and rocked it, singing a lullaby recounting the whole incident. Sage Atri, who was on his way home, heard the song from a distance and knew what had transpired. On reaching the hermitage, he glorified the Trinity thus: "Oh, Thou Supreme Spirit! You are the ultimate cause of creation, preservation and destruction. You are the witness of the whole universe, the omnipresent, all-pervading essence of all existence. You are Lord Vishnu. You are indeed the reality. But by Your divine sport, you manifested as the holy Trinity for Your own play. Though the universe is a projection of nescience of your Real Essence, it is not distinct from you. Only when perceived through the illusory sense of 'I and mine', it looks distinct from you."

As he said thus, even while the three infant forms were in front of him, they also appeared before him in their original forms and wanted him to seek as boon from them. He then looked meaningfully at his wife and said, "MY dear, these holy ones cannot be reached even by the mind. They appeared here only by the power of your devotion. Tell them of your heart's wish." She replied, "My Lord, you were created by Brahma for the promotion of the phenomenon of creation. Therefore, I shall be pleased if you pray to the one Lord that has appeared as this Trinity to live as our son." Sage Atri did so. So the one Spirit, manifest as the trio said, "Oh wise sage, I offer Myself to you henceforth as your adopted Son, Hence I am Datta." (*Datta* means the adopted son In Sanskrit

In order to denote that Datta was his son, he came to be known as Dattatreya. He is indeed the Supreme Lord Himself, the goal of the *Vedas*. He is of the nature of Reality-Awareness-Bliss. He is the master of *yoga* and wisdom, the wish-fulfiller of His devotees and wandering all over the creation ever ready to bless them at their mere thought of Him.

The Supreme Spirit, henceforth known as Dattatreya, is indeed unbound by phenomenal existence. Yet, in deference to a curse laid on Him once by Sage Durvasa, He ever abides on earth, assuming different human forms. This He does out of compassion for the creatures on earth and for the gods. Thus Dattatreya is the eternal *Avatar* of God's spirit and self-dedication to the salvation of all creatures. He manifests Himself perennially as the perfect saint of all religious of the world.

Sri Shirdi Sai Baba is believed to be the third prominent incarnation of Dattatreya. It is said that His contemporary saint, Swami Samarth of Akkalkot (1800-1878), was also an incarnation of Dattatreya. The essence of Sai-Datta philosophy is the oneness of the individual soul with the universal soul.

Iconographically, Dattatreya is shown surrounded by animals including dogs that also figure in the symbolism of Sai Baba. It may be recalled that dogs were favourites of Shirdi Sai Baba. At Shirdi even now it is considered to be an act of religious piety on the part of Sai devotees to offer milk to the dogs near the famous Dwarka Mai Masjid of Shirdi Sai Baba. In many pictures of Shirdi Sai Baba, a dog is shown seated near Him. Many devotees had experienced that Baba often went to their houses when invited for lunch, in the form of a dog; many a time the hosts discarded or hit the dog out of their ignorance not realizing that Baba was present in all creatures including those dogs.

As a Great Saint, *Nath* or *Pir* in the *Naathpanthi* Tradition of Saivite Ascetics

In the sacred and most authentic book, *Shri Sai Sat Charita* or *The Wonderful Life* and *Teachings of Sri Sai Baba* (English translation), the English translator, Nagesh Vasudev Gunaji, has written that Sri Shirdi Sai Baba was chief of the Nath-Panchayatan at that time:

"It is said that a few centuries ago, there was a *Daspanchayatan* (group of five saints) consisting of Samarth Ramdas, Jayaramaswami, Ranganathaswami, Keshavaswami and Anandamurth. Similarly, it is said that there was *Nath-Panchayatan* in those days, consisting of Madhavnath Sri Sadguru Sainath, Dunddiraj Palusi, Gajanan Maharaj of Shegaum, and Gopaldas (Narsing Maharaj) of Nasik and they all worked together by inner control or force. One Suman Sunser has also written about this in *Sai Leela* where in he says that Sai Nath (Baba) had great respect in this *Panchayatan* and was referred to as *Trilokinath* and *Kohinoor* by Madhavnath.

According to Professor Charles S.J. White, Associate Professor of Philosophy and Religion at the American University, Washington D.C., "Gorakhnath's order is peculiar and significant in relation to the Sai Baba movement for several reasons. There is evidence that the *Nathpanthis* have some connection with Islamic asceticism. . . a principal focus of the community and religious life in a *Nathpanthi* house is the hearth or *dhuni* wherein a fire is kept perpetually burning."

Prof. White adds, "Sai Baba was a celibate, remaining in one place, performing miracles, admonishing his disciples and keeping a fire perpetually burning in a *dhuni*. Therefore, it would not be unreasonable to assume that he was following customs already sanctified in the *Nathpanthi* tradition with its own degree of Muslim-Hindu assimilation. The *Nathpanthi yogis* are well known in the Shirdi region and the picture of their founders can be purchased at the Shirdi Shrine."

Nathpanthi saints were famous for their *siddhis* (power to do miracles). Shirdi Sai Baba also had exhibited a number of such powers. *Shri Sai Sat Charita* and several other books on the life and miracles of Sri Shirdi Sai Baba are full of numerous incidents in which Baba used His *siddhis* for the welfare of His devotees. Like *Guru* Gorakhnath, Shirdi Sai Baba was also using the ash (*udi* or *vibhuti*) of the *dhuni* established by Him to cure His devotees of all kinds of illnesses and miseries.

As Incarnation of Kabir

Sri Shirdi Sai Baba had revealed to one of His close devotees that in one of His several incarnations, He was Kabir, the famous saint of the *Bhakti* (meditation) period of the medieval Indian history. Kabir's teacher was saint Ramanand of Varanasi. It is believed that the same Guru Ramanand was reborn as *Guru* Venkusha of Sailu under whose care and guidance Shirdi Sai Baba lived and imbibed spirituality from the age of 4 to 16 (1842 to 1854).

It is on record that while giving His evidence in a case related to a devotee before a Commission of Enquiry, Shirdi Sai Baba had stated that His creed or religion was Kabir. No one knows for sure whether Kabir was bron a Hindu or a Muslim but he was a weaver by profession and his life and teaching are most inspiring.

In his article "Kabir: the Iconoclast", eminent scholar Dr. Gopal Singh had thrown this valuable light on the great saint:

"Such utter contempt Kabir shows for the rituals and superstitious beliefs and so devastating he is in his criticism of the age-old religious practices and dogmas of both the Hindu and Muslim that one is in fact *dazzled* by the boldness of his spiritual insights and the freshness of metaphor.

Kabir is the worshipper of one God, both absolute and manifest in his creation. He can be attained, he says, through pure conduct and meditation, but through no ritual is He pleased, nor by high caste or station. The realization comes through one's illumination within, and not by performing pilgrimages, or offering oblations, propitiating the Brahmins or the Mullahs or performing the Haj, or by repeating the text of the books considered sacred by the devout.

He ridicules the superstitious beliefs with ruthlessness unheard of in the mystic compositions of anyone before him:

> If one attains *yoga* by roaming about naked,
> Then the deer in the woods would all be emancipated!
> If by close-cropping the hair, one becomes a *siddha*,
> Then all the shorn sheep would find deliverance forthwith!
> O friend, if one were to be redeemed by celibacy,
> Then all the eunuchs would be in the highest state of bliss!
> They who bathe morning and evening (to wash off their sins)
> Are no better than frogs who live constantly in the water!
> He makes no distinction between the Hindus and Muslims and
> argues against the rituals of both as is evident from his following
> songs:
> Wherefrom have the Hindus come?
> Wherefrom the Muslims?
> Who created the two Paths?
> O man of evil intent, reflect this in your mind;
> Who, pray, is the creator of Heaven and Hell?

According to Kabir, it is the pure conduct which avails one in the end, and not the beliefs which one holds or practices . . . it is through contentment, right conduct, truthful living and compassion that God is attained, not through falsehood, greed and violence. The householder must observe the rules of moral conduct as much as a recluse foregoes desire and sensuous tastes. The recluse or the devotee, however, is not to be denied his daily necessities; it is, therefore in the fitness of things that Kabir demands from God all the wherewithal's of a cultured life. He has no use for a God who keeps him famished and hungry, and yet demands devotion and dedication from him."

Kabir said, "for the man who realizes God, the distinctions of creed, caste or color disappear and he sees the One alone in all." Kabir is thus the Guru of the modern enlightened world, which seeks to fight fundamentalism, superstition, but cannot and yet seek spiritual illumination and love for all.

Shirdi Sai Baba's teachings and style of functioning greatly resembled Kabir. It is of interest that in the *sakhis* and *dohas* of Kabir, the word "Sai" (meaning God) was used at some places. As a matter of fact, the earliest use of the word 'Sai' in Hindi language was found only in the compositions of Kabir.

Sai Baba's *Dwarka Mai* masjid welcomed both the Hindus and Muslims as well as others in a perfectly secular and tolerant manner. Like Kabir, Baba tried to teach the basics of spiritually to all people in a plain, straightforward and simple manner. However, there was a difference: while Kabir ridiculed the established religious traditions and rituals like idol worship, reading of sacred texts, establishment of temples and mosques, traditional modes of worship, etc., Sai Baba did not do so. In the spirit of secularism and tolerance, He allowed His devotees to stick to their chosen gods and goddesses, traditional modes of worship and acts of charity like giving *dakshina* or *dan*, feeding the hungry and all such things. This prominently positive and integrative approach won for Him a unique veneration and love of people of all communities despite His often curt, impolite and abusive speech and His beating the devotees in moods of feigned anger. It may thus be said that Sai Baba was an improved model of Kabir suited to the socio-cultural context of the latter half of the 19th century and the early two decades of the 20th century. The *siddhis* or miracle – making powers displayed by Him so frequently and effortlessly and boons given to barren women, diseased, poor and unfortunate people and deliverance from the cycle of birth and death to several people as well as animals and, above all, His frequent revelations about innumerable past births of men, women, children, creatures like snakes, frogs, dogs, buffaloes, tigers etc., made Him all the more adorable, loving and far more impressive than His past incarnation as Kabir.

Whereas Kabir emerged as a radical and iconoclastic spiritualist in the mould of a religious reformer, Sai Baba truly projected Himself as an all embracing, kind, bountiful, omnipresent, omnipotent and omniscient God eager to help His devotes of all faiths, materially as well as spiritually. While Kabir laid emphasis only on the nirakar (formless) God, Baba was more pragmatic than him, for He felt that the rural and traditional folk could comprehend the *nirakar* only after they had seen a *sakar* God in the form of statues as well as in the from of his living personality as an incarnation of God.

Professor White, in the course of philosophical research on the Sai Baba movement, tried to correlate *Nathpanthis*, Kabir and Sai Baba in a common bond of linkage. According to him:

"It is not known precisely whether he (Kabir) was born a Muslim or a Hindu but Charlotte Vaudeville is of the view that he belonged to a *jati* which had been converted from Hinduism to Islam in fairly recent times and had called themselves Yogis and lived a householder's life. Although a Hindu, apparently by choice, and a theist, he taught an extreme form of devotion to God without qualities; he also referred to God of his inner experience as the *Guru*. There is some evidence that he had been trained but had rejected the type of Yoga practiced int eh Nathpanthi order and there is even a tradition that he and Gorakhnath had met. Kabir's humble origin, his love for all mankind whether Hindu, Muslim or otherwise, his reputed affection for animals, his yogic connections (perhaps with the Nathpanthi order) and the uniquely synthetic character of his religious position point the direction toward the founder of the Sai Baba movement.

In *Shri Sai Sat Charita*', Hemadpant described the well known incident of Baba grinding wheat in order to prevent cholera epidemic from affecting Shirdi. After describing that incident, the author recalls a similar story connected with Kabir:

This reminds us of a similar story of Kabir who seeing a woman grinding corn said to his guru, Nipathiranjan, "I am weeping because I feel the agony of being crushed in this wheel of worldly existence like the corn in the hand mill." Nipathiranjan replied, "Do not be afraid; hold fast to the handle of knowledge of this mill, as I do, and do not wander away from the same but turn inward to the centre, and you are sure to be saved."

Along with these interesting theories, it must be noted that Baba Himself disclosed that He was always present, His age was "lakhs of years", His caste or community was *Parvardigar* (God) and He had taken innumerable incarnations. He informed His devotee Shama that He had been with him for the last 74 births. He informed Narke and Hemadpant and several other devotees about their past lives. He told one of his devotees that He had lived at Shirdi thousands of years earlier also and that his Guru's *Samadhi* was located under a particular *neem* tree. the Gurusthan (Teacher's place) is there, which is venerated as a very holy spot in Shirdi by all devotees.

Baba's Other Incarnations

Baba once recalled that in one of His births in the fifteenth century when He was a Muslim *fakir* and had gone to meet a Brahmin Yogi, Mukund Brahmachari who did not welcome Him. Then at the market place, He saw a young royal couple, emperor Humanyun and his wife Hamida, in exile with three attendants. They were begging for water and the *Fakr* gave the water from His *Kamandalu* (vessel), and blessed the couple that a son would be born to them and He would be a king of India. That child became Akbar. Mukund Brahamachari soon thereafter died and reincarnated as Akbar, as per Baba's prophecy.

Baba once told His devotees, Khaparde and his wife, that both of them had contacts with each other in many previous lives. He told Khaparde that they had been His kinsmen in a former life, had lived together for about two or three years, as wealthy persons, and after some years Khaparde had left His company and gone to a distant place to serve as a king.Thus we can understand that Sai Baba has been appearing at different times.

Origin

There are two popular sayings in our country:

"A *Sadhu* has no caste".

"One should not try to find the origin of a river or a saint".

It is far more important for us to know the message or contribution of great saints than to know about their family history, circumstances of birth etc. But as a human beings with curiosity as one of our basic instincts, we cannot resist the temptation or curiosity of trying to discover the family background and circumstances of the birth of saints.

When Sri Shirdi Sai Baba was alive (1838-1918), no one actually knew or could tell with any measure of authority about the parentage, circumstances of birth and early childhood of Baba. The villagers of Shirdi and the contemporary devotees could not say with certainty whether Baba was a Hindu or a Muslim. Baba Himself did not disclose it, as He did not want His devotees to bother about knowing His background. He was more concerned about the establishment of Hindu-Muslim unity and about the welfare and spiritual elevation of His devotees, rather than establishing and promoting a personality for Himself.

However, the testimonies of some of His close devotees like Mlahaspati, Abdul, Das Ganu, Shama, Sai Sharananad, etc., reveal that Baba had certainly given a number of crucial hints very casually about His origin and early childhood. The following hints given by Him are thus relevant:

- An extract from *Shri Sai Sat Charita*:

'Mlahaspati, an intimate devotee of Shirdi Sai Baba, who always slept with Him in the *Masjid* and *chavadi*, said that Sai Baba had told him that he was a Brahmin of Pathri and was handed over to a *faqir* in His infancy. When He told this, some men from Pathri had come and Baba was enquiring about some people from that place."

- Mrs. Kashibai Kanitkar, the famous learned Sai devotee of Poona, revealed her experience published in *Sai Leela*:

"On hearing of Baba's miracles, we were discussing according to our theosophic convention and fashion whether Sai Baba belonged to the Black or White Lodge. When once I went to Shirdi, I was thinking seriously about this in my mind. As soon as I approached the steps of *Masjid*, Baba came to the front and pointing to His chest and staring at me spoke rather vehemently – "This is a Brahmin, pure Brahmin. He has nothing to do with black things. No Musalman can dare step in here. He dare not." Again pointing to His chest, he said "This Brahmin alone can bring lakhs on the white path and take them to their destination. This is a Brahmin's *Masjid* and I won't allow any black Mohammedan to cast His shadow here."

- Baba told Sharananad also in 1912 that He was Brahmin.
- In his testimony, Das Ganu, a close devotee of Baba, stated that Baba revealed the following facts about Him to Nana joshi, commissioner sent by Dhulia Court to Baba to examine Him in a trial case concerning a thief who had been charged with the theft of jewels:
  Commissioner (C): What is your name?
  B: Sai Baba

C: Your father's name?

Baba(B) Also Sai Baba.

C:Your *Guru's* name?

B:Venkusha.

C:Creed or Religion?

B:Kabir.

C:Caste or Race?

B:*Parvardigar* (God).

- *Shri Sai Satcharita* records Mrs. Radhabai Deshmukh's experience. Baba toldher:

"I resorted to my *Guru* for 12 years. He brought me up. There was no dearth of food and clothing. He was full of love, nay He was love incarnate. How can I describe it? I love Him the most. Rare is a *Guru* like him.

Early in October 1918, Baba's most favourite possession, a brick, which was His *Guru's* parting gift to Him in 1854 fell down from the hands of the boy, Madhav Fasle, in Dwarka Mai *Masjid* and broke. Baba was very much depressed to see it and said, "It is not the brick that is broken; it is my destiny. It has been my lifelong companion and I meditated on the self with its help; it is my very life. It has left me today. I shall not survive for long."

Shri Sai Sat Charita also records this incident:

"In 1916, on the *Vijayadashmi (Dussehra)* Baba suddenly got into wild rage in the evening when people were returning from *'Seemallanghan'* (crossing the border or limits of the village). Taking off His head-dress, *Kafni* and *langota*, etc., He tore them and threw them in the *dhuni* before them. Fed by this offering, the fire in the *dhuni* began to burn brighter and Baba shone still brighter. He stood there stark naked and with His burning red eyes shouted, "You fellows, now have a look and decide finally whether I am a Muslim or a Hindu.

The devotees looked at the Baba and found that He had not been circumcised and, therefore, He was not a Muslim but a Hindu. It was also discovered by Baba's devotees that His earlobes had been pierced as is the custom in the Hindus."

- Baba had once told His devotees that He was given to a *faqir* by His parents in His childhood. These hints had given the broad idea to most of His contemporary devotees that Baba was a Brahmin by birth and was trained under a Brahmin *Guru* Venkusha, but they did not know anything more than this. During the last two decades, three valuable sources of information about Sri Shirdi Baba's origin and childhood have emerged:

- Research finding of V.N. Kher.
- Revelations of Sri Sathya Sai Baba, who claimed himself to be the incarnation of Sri Shirdi Sai Baba.
- The memoirs of Shivamma Thayee, 104 years old lady, an old devotee of Shirdi Sai Baba.

Research Findings of V.N. Kher

V.N. Kher, a noted Gandhian and an ardent Sai Devotee, went to Pathri village in 1975 to discover the facts of Shirdi Sai Baba's family background. He did extensive investigation contacting each Brahmin family in the village. He had detailed discussions with one Professor Raghunath Bhusari, a retired professor of Marathi at the Osmania University, Hyderabad, who was believed o be a member of Shirdi Sai Baba's clan.

Kher's research findings are:

The Brahmins of Pathri are all Desatha Brahmins – either Rigvedi or Yajurvedi; there are no Brahmins of any other sub-caste. The family deity of almost all the Brahmin families of Pathri is either Goddess Renuka Mahur or Yogeswari of Ambajogai. There is only one exception, that of Bhusari family whose family deity is Hanuman of *Kumhar-bavadi* on the outskirts of Pathri village. Kuner Dada was the first known ancestor of this Bhusari clan of Brahmins of Pathri. No information was available about the next two generations. Then there was one Parsuram. He had five sons – Raghupati, Dada, Haribhau, Ambadas and Balwant. Haribhau, Ambadas and Balwant had left Pathri for good. Haribhau might have gone in search of God, while the other two went to seek their fortunes elsewhere. In all probability, Haribhau Bhusari later on became known as Sai Baba of Shirdi. The House No. 4-438-61 in Vaishnav Gali near *Kumhar-bavadi* in Pathri village, which was in ruins when V.B. Kher visited it in 1975, was identified as the family house of Sai Baba. This has now been taken over by the local Sai Samiti for Shirdi Sai Temple where prayers are held every Thursday.

Kher's findings certainly are interesting. One of the most important findings hat Sai Baba's clan worshipped Hanuman has great significance. In the course of our own research on Sri Shirdi Sai Baba, we have discovered the following evidence:

It has been reported by several devotees who had seen Baba that He used to pay special regards to Hanuman.In his early years at Shirdi (1958-78) Baba used to visit Maruti (Hanuman) Temple close to His *Dwarka Mai Masjid* so very often and meet saint Devidas who used to live there, and the two used to talk for hours.Baba had got the Maruti Temple renovated at His own cost and inspiration.While going to *Chavadi* every alternate evening and while returning from *Chavadi* to *Dwarka Mai Masjid* the next morning in the procession, Baba used to stop for a moment, look invariably towards the Hanuman (Maruti) Temple and make some mysterious spiritual gestures towards it. This has been reported by many contemporary devotees.Baba's love and regards for Hanuman and Rama were well known to most of His contemporary devotees.

Sri Sathya Sai Baba's revealations about Shirdi Sai Baba:

Sri Sathya Sai Baba on 23rd May, 1940 had revealed that He was Sai Baba – reincarnation of Sri Shirdi Sai Baba and this has een very widely accepted by millions of devotees throughout the world.In 1974, Sri Sathya Sai Baba revealed some unknown facts about the birth and childhood of Sri Shirdi Sai Baba's incarnation and His own previous life to Professor V.K. Gokak, Professor S. Bhagvantam and some others. Professor Gokak recorded those revelations in his Foreward to T.S. Anantha Murthy's book Life and Teachings of Sri Sai Baba and told him and others in 1974 about Sri Shirdi Sai Baba's birth and childhood and they are reproduced below:

"Sai Baba of Shirdi was the third child of a boatman, Ganga Bavadia, who lived in Pathri, a village near Manmad, on the banks of a river. His (Sri Sai Baba's) mother's name was Devagiriamma. On a certain night when the river was in spate, the boatman Ganga Bavadia, who had all his boats moored to the bank, was scared that they might be swept away by the swirling waters. He went to the riverside, leaving his wife alone at home. At that time, an old man came and asked Devagiriamma to give him food. She served him food in the verandah.

He then asked for permission to sleep there as he had nowhere to go. She permitted him to sleep in the verandah. After a little while, she heard somebody tapping at the door. It was the old man again. He said that he could not sleep. He desired that a lady should massage his legs. Devagiriamma went at that hour of the night by the back door to the houses of one or two courtesans, but could not find any of them at home. She was bewildered and did not know what to do. She was a devotee of Goddess Parvati and her husband was a devotee of *Easwara* (Shiva). She sat in her worship-room and prayed and cried bitterly.

At that moment, she heard a knock on the back-door. As she opened the door, she saw a woman standing there who said that she was from one of those houses that Devagiriamma had visited and she wanted to know what could she do for her. Devagiriamma was overcome with joy and she took the woman to the old man in the verandah and closed the door on both of them. After a while, she heard another tap on the verandah door. She thought that the woman probably wanted to return home, so she opened the door. What did she see there? Lord Shiva and Goddess Parvati were themselves standing there, ready to bless her.

Goddess Parvati said to Shiva, "Let us together bless her." Shiva replied, "Since I came here to test her, I will speak to her separately." Devagiriamma was childless till then. Goddess Parvati blessed her and said, "Be the mother of two children." Devagiriamma bowed to Shiva, who said to her, "I will be born as your third child, a son." By the time Devagiriamma looked up, the Divine pair had vanished.

When the husband (Ganga Bavadia) came home in the early hours of the morning, Devagiriamma narrated all her strange experiences to him. He was incredulous and thought it all to be the result of an over-heated brain, as she had been left alone at home on a stormy night. But the events that followed did prove the veracity of her experiences. Devagiriamma became the mother of two children and it was soon clear that she would become the mother of third child also.

But an unusual situation developed on the domestic front. The husband gradually lost all his interest in mundane things and was pining to meet God face to face. When his wife reminded him all that the Divine couple had told her had come true and Shiva himself would now be born as their child, he said, "Even if it be so, it will not satisfy me. There will be the mask of human child between me and God. I want to seek that unmitigated primordial splendour", and set out on his quest. Torn between her husband and her children. Devagiriamma decided that it was her duty to follow her husband footsteps, so she went her two children to her mother's home and accompanied her husband into the forest.

After they had covered some distance, Devagiriamma felt that she was soon going to give birth to a child because the birth pains had started. She implored her husband to wait for a while, but he kept going his way. As soon as she was delivered of the baby boy, beneath the shade of banyan tree, she placed her child on the ground, covered it with banyan leaves and hastened after her husband, for her duty lay in that direction. Bloodstains were still visible on the child's tender body and one could make out that it was born only a few minutes earlier.

This is how destiny works. A person named 'Patil' from a neighbouring villag was fetching his wife from her mother's hamlet, in a *tonga* (horse carriage). At that very spot, his wife felt like answering a call of nature. Mr. Patil asked the tonga-driver to stop for a while.

Mrs. Patil alighted from the tonga and went to the very spot where the child had been made to lie by Devagiriamma. She heard the child's cry, removed the leaves and found that it was a newborn child. Excited, she called her husband to the spot and showed him the child. They were a childless couple and it was their in start belief that God had blessed them with that child. They took the child home and brought it up as their own son."

On 28 September 1990, and then on 27 September 1992, Sri Sathya Sai Baba gave two full-fledged discourses on the life of Sri Shirdi Sai Baba. In these discourses, He repeated almost all the above account and added the following facts of great interest:

- Devagiriamma had mixed some flour with curds and given it as food to the old man [Lord Shiva].
- Parvati then blessed her (Devagiriamma): "I grant you a son to maintain the lineage and a daughter for *kanya-ka-dan* (a girl to be offered in marriage).
- She (Devagiriamma) delivered the boy. Wrapping the by in a piece of cloth, she left the child by the roadside and followed her husband.
- Shirdi Sai Baba was born on 27 September 1938.

An analysis of the above facts provide us the following us the following conclusion:

To some extent, the information given by V.B. Kher about Sri Shirdi Sai Baba's parentage seems to be correct, particularly the one that Baba's parents were Desatha Yajurvedi Brahmins whose family deity was Hanuman of *Kumhar-bavadi* on the outskirts of Pathri village. Kher has stated that Parsuram had five sons and the third one 'Haribhau' was perhaps the one who later became Sai Baba of Shirdi. But Sri Sathya Sai Baba mentioned Ganga Bavadia as the father of Shirdi Sai Baba, and added that after the birth of one son and one daughter Shirdi Sai Baba was born to Devagiriamma, wife of Ganga Bavadia.) It is possible that Parsuram might have been the childhood name and Ganga the adulthood name of Shirdi Sai Baba's father. It is customary in Hindu families to change one's childhood name when a boy or girl becomes somewhat grown up and starts going out.It is likely that Raghupati and Dada might be names of the two children who died in their infancy in the early years of married life of Devagiriamma. Then three children including the youngest one Haribhau might have been born to her as per boon granted to her by Shakti and Shiva. Kher mentions the names Haribhau, Ambadas, Balwant; perhaps instead of them and in that order, the three later children of Devagiriamma were Ambadas, a girl (May be Balwant Bai or so) and Haribhau. If this is correct, then one can say that the findings of Kher and revelations of Sri Sathya Sai Baba come very close as real facts. At any rate, we are inclined to believe in what Sri Sathya Sai Baba has revealed.Kher's findings that Sri Shirdi Sai Baba belonged to Bhusari family of Pathri to which Professor Raghunath Bhusari belongs and the surname *'Bhavadia'* of Baba's father Ganga can be accepted. Actually, it should be *'Bavadia'* i.e., one who lives near a *bavadi* (natural water pond) in a village. Kher has mentioned that Sai Baba's ancestral family lived in a house near *Kumar Bavadi* (the pondo f the *Kumhars*, i.e., potters), and all its members were the worshippers of Hanuman whose temple was located there.

On the basis of these circumstantial evidences, we may assume that in all probability the child was born at noon, say between 12 noon and 1.30 p.m. or so. The reasons for estimating the time of birth to the near the noon are that the parents of Baba might have left their house in Pathri early in the morning of 27 September 1838, at about 5 a.m. or so; they might have covered the distance of 4-5 miles on foot by say 11 a.m. since Devagiriamma, was in a very advanced stage of pregnancy; *Fakir* Patil and his wife *Fakiri* might have reached spot in the forest at or slightly after 12 noon, since it is customary in the Indian families to allow a married girl and her husband to leave the girl's parental home only after lunch. They might have covered a distance of 7-8 miles through the forest in about 2 hours. If they left Patil's house after lunch at 10 a.m. they might have reached that spot near the banyan tree in the forest around 1 p.m. Based on these assumptions, it would be fair to assess that Baba's birth time should be 12 noon or so, about 40-50 minutes before the arrival of Patil's *tonga*(horse cart)/I was informed by (late) Raghunathn of Chennai that he had found out from anancient nasdi in Chennai that he was the eldler brother of Sai Baba and Baba Patti was Baba's mother in their past life.

Childhood

Sojournings
Events of 1854

After leaving His *Guru's ashram* at Sailu, one evening in early 1854, most probably after Shivaratri in February 1854, Babu, the young saint, attired as a Muslim *faqir* with *kafni* (head-dress) walked all alone with the brick and loin cloth gifted to Him by Venkusha.It seems that He did not go to Shirdi directly. The following disclosure by Baba to His devotees, Bade Baba and Bapugir Gasavi, as recorded by Gawankar, is revealing:

"I grew up (lived) in Mahugarh (a holy place of lord Dattatreya): when people pestered Me, I left for Girnar, there too people troubled Me much so I left for Mount Abu (in Rajasthan). There too the same thing happened. Then I came to Akkalkot and from there to Daulatabad. Then Janardana Swami (a great saint) did Me lot of *seva* (service). Then I went to Pandharpur; from there I came to Shirdi."

This shows that Baba first of all reached Mahugarh from Sailu and stayed there for some weeks. It also shows that He must have taken moths in going to so many places, so He might have in all probability reached Shirdi in September 1854 or so.

First Visit to Shirdi

The 16-year-old handsome boy attired as a Muslim *fakir* travelled to Shirdi *on* foot. He perhaps wanted to stay in Khandoba Temple, but out of orthodoxy the priest of that temple, Mlahaspati, did not allow Him to do so. So He took shelter under a *neem* (margasa) tree outside Shirdi village on the other side of

Khandoba Temple which was in an isolated place near a jungle of *babul* shrubs at that time.He dug out a pit at the foot of the *neem* (margosa) tree and for most of the time sat hidden in that pit. Baba later on disclosed that He had been undergoing penance or mediation in that pit, the passage from which led to a long dark cave. He lived the life of recluse, seldom visible to people. The first person to see Him was Mlahaspat who felt attracted by His magnetic, youthful and silent personality and also got His two close friends, Kashinath Sipmi (a tailor and a cloth merchant) and Jogle, interested in the young *faqir*. One peasant couple, Appa Patil Kote and his wife Bayjabai who met Him, were also very much impressed by His Godly personality. Bayjabai then and there decided to take up the vow of giving Him *roti*(bread at lunch every day and herself eating her lunch only after that. She used to search for the young *fakir* (who never disclosed His name) in the nearby fields and jungle and feed Him with motherly love.

The young *fakir* sometimes begged for food in the village – once, twice or more, or sometimes not at all. Sai Sharnananda has written that Baba had disclosed to him in 1910 that He used to live under that neem tree all alone doing penance as the tomb of one of His previous lives was located there. After years of such penance in the cave, people caught sight of Him one day when He came out for water. It seemed He had finished His tenure of penance because thereafter He did not return to the cave..

There exists a recorded testimony describing the 16 years old young Baba under that *neem* tree in 1854: Nana Chopdar's mother, an old lady, had seen this young *faqir* one day and she portrayed Him in these words:

"This young lad, fair, smart and very handsome, was first seen under the *neem* tree, seated in *asana* (yogic posture). The people of the village were wonderstruck to see such a young lad practicing hard penance, not minding heat and cold. By day he associated with none, by night he was afraid of none. Outwardly he looked very young but by his actions He was really a great soul. He was the embodiment of dispassion and was an enigma to all.'

The young *fakir* told Mlahaspati and His friends decided that the place where He stayed under the *neem* tree, being the tomb of His *Guru* of previous birth, was a sacred place and so it should be kept safe, clean, plastered with cow dung, and *loban* (incense) should be burnt on it. Mlahaspati and His friends agreed to do so. Assuring them thus, one night He slipped out of

Shirdi without informing anybody. He had stayed there hardly for two months.

Events during 1854-1858

It seems that Baba left Shirdi in November 1854 or so. What He did during his *agyatvas* (period of disguised wanderings) of about three and a half or four years, i.e. till 1958, is still shrouded in mystery. However, a close perusal of *'Shri Sai Sat Charita', 'Devotees', Experience of Sri Sai Baba', Khaparde's ;Shirdi Diary'* and some other valuable books have enabled us to discover some of the valuable hints given by Baba to some of His close devotees with regard to the events of His life during these four mysterious years, and on that basis, the order of those events can be reconstructed as under:

On 30 December, 1911, Shirdi Sai Baba told some devotees including Khaparde that He had stayed at Aurangabad with a *faqir* for sometime. Khaparde recorded it in his *Shirdi Diary* as under:

"He (Sri Sai Baba) said that He had gone to Aurangabad in one of His wanderings and had seen a *faqir* sitting in a Masjid near which there was a very tall temrind tree. The *faqir* did not allow Him to enter the Masjid at first but ultimately consented to His putting up in it. The *faqir* depended entirely on a piece of *roti* (cake) which an old woman used to supply him at midday. He (Baba) volunteered to beg for him and kept him supplied amply with food for four years and then thought of leaving the place. The *faqir* shed tears and had to be consoled with soft words. Sai Maharaj visited him four years later and found him there doing well. The *faqir* then came here (Shirdi) a few years ago and lodged at *Chawdi*. From what he said I gathered that Sai Baba stayed for twelve years to instruct the Aurangabad *faqir* and set him up fully in the spiritual world."

It seems that the *fakir* with whom Baba had stayed in the Aurangabad mosque and served him was Bade Baba or *faqir* Meer Mohammad Yasin Mian or Malegaon Baba *faqir*, who had in his very old age come to stay with Sri Sai Baba at Shirdi and whom Baba used to give the highest amount of daily gift out of His day's collection of *dakshina* (alms) from visitors and devotees. Baba met him after four years, which means He had visited him at Aurangabad again in 1858 some weeks before His reaching Shirdi. It, however, appears that Khaparde also perhaps did not hear or understand the Baba's revelation correctly. Baba might have mentioned just 'twelve' or 'twelve months', not 'twelve years', for how could He stay at Aurangabad for 12 years when the duration between His two visits to Shirdi was just less than four years?

It is evident from the following disclosure by Baba to some of the devotees that He had worked for about 10-12 months in 1856:

"When I was a youngster, I was in search of bread and butter I went to Badgaum. There I got an embroidery work. I worked hard, sparing no pains. The employer was very much pleased with me. Three other boys had worked before me. The first got Rs.50/- the second Rs.100/- and I was given twice the whole of this amount. Seeing my cleverness, the employer presented me with a full dress, a turban for the head and a *shella* for the body, etc. I kept this dress intact without using it. I thought that what a man might give does not last long and is imperfect but what my *Sircar* (God) gives lasts to the end of time."

Baba once casually disclosed to Upasani Maharaj's elder brother on his first visit to Shirdi on 31 December 1911 that He had been at the battle in which the Rani of Jhansi took part. He was then in her army. It is widely known that Rani Laxmi Bai of Jhansi was an important leader of the First War of India's Independence in 1857. She had fought against the British rulers of India and laid her life in the battle. It is possible that Baba under some other name might have been employed as a casual soldier in the army of Rani Laxmi Bai at Jhansi, or in one of her army units fighting the British near Aurangabad, Nagpur or Khandwa. However, Sholapurkar in *Footprints at Shirdi and Puttaparthi* has conjectured that He might have joined the army of Nana Saheb Peshwa at Bithur (near Kanpur) in Uttar Pradesh, who was an ally of Rani Laxmi Bai, but this does not appear to be correct. Most probably, Baba was employed in the army of Rani Jhansi which was fighting one of the battles with the British in the vicinity of Jhansi itself in 1857. After the martyrdom of Rani Jhansi, her army got disbanded, and then Baba might have left the army and again donned His earlier dress and lifestyle of a Muslim *fakir* in order to hide His identity as a erstwhile soldier of the Rani Jhansi's army.

He might have then visited on foot His native place passing through Pathri, the village of His birth, Sailu, the place of His Guru Venkusha's *ashram* and other places. This is evident from the following disclosure by Baba to some of His contemporary devotees:

"The path was from Pathri. From there Shillud (Sailu), Manoor (Manvat) and Jalnapur. I had been once (by that route). It took Me eight days. By day I trod over the grass and slept at night in the grass. We walked step by step.

Kamath and Kher here add: 'Thus Baba reached Paithan-Aurangabad' where He stayed for twelve years in a mosque and guided a *fakir*."

The first half of the above statement seems to be correct, but the other half is totally incorrect. Baba certainly revisited Bade Baba at the Mosque at Paithan in Aurangabad in 1857 or early 1858 to enquire about his welfare, as Baba's revelation to Khaparde on 30 December, 1911 shows. He might have stayed there with him for a few days, but His stay there for twelve years in certainly incorrect.

Then we come across a valuable testimony of a businessman of Rahata Amool Chand Sait (Seth), with whose elder cousin, Khushal Chand, Baba later developed great friendship:

My elder cousin Kushal Bhav, who died on 5-11-1918, told me that previously Sai Baba lived with Muslim saint Ali (Akbar Ali perhaps) whose portrait is kept in our *gin*, i.e. *Rahatekar Gin* near Wadia Park at Ahmednagar, and Dalu Sait (Son of Kushal Chand Sait) had seen Baba with the saint at Ahmednagar and that Baba came from Ahmednagar to live at Rahata and then went to live at Shirdi.

This evidence shows that Baba lived for sometime – may be for a few months – with the Muslim *faqir* Akbar Ali at Ahmednagar in 1858, but the latter part of the evidence "that Baba came to live at Rahata and then went to live at Shirdi" does not seem to be in order.

After leaving Ahmednagar, Baba was wandering. One day, He was seated under a mango tree by side of the path in the forest near the twin villages of Bindhon-Sindhon, 24 Kms from Aurangabad. Here Chand Bhai Patil (Patel), a well-off resident of Dhoop KHeda village, met Him (young Faqir Sai Baba). Chand Bhai was wandering with a horse saddle on his shoulders and seemed to be tired and worried. Baba called him by name and greatly impressed him as a divine personality by doing three miracles with a few minutes – showing his lost mare grazing under a tree nearby in the forest. Materializing live embers from the ground by thrusting His tongs, and materializing water then and there for wetting the piece of cloth needed for smoking His *chilam* (clay pipe). This thrilling incident of the meeting of Chand Bhai Patil with the young Baba in 1858 is very widely mentioned in all books on Sai Baba and also in the Hindi Film *Shirdi Ke Sai Baba*.

In some books, it is mentioned that on Chand Bhai's request, Baba went with him to his village Dhoopkheda on the same day. In some other books, it is mentioned that Baba did not go with him on that very day, but He said that He would reach his village after 2-3 days. The latter seems to be correct for Chand Bhai did not ever tell anyone at Shirdi during his lifetime that Baba had rode His mare along with him on His return journey to Dhoop Kheda. Kamath and Kher are of the view that Baba reached Dhoopkheda all alone after a few days to accept the hospitality of a grateful new devotee, Chand Bhai Patil; this seems to be perfectly correct.

Sholapurkar has recorded this thrilling incident of Baba's visit to Dhoopkheda:

When Baba went to Dhoop Kheda along with Chand Bhai, He threw stones at the advancing crowd who would not allow the two to proceed further. This behavior of the crowd threw Baba in tantrums and He hurled stones all round. The crowd became panicky and ran helter-skelter. A stone, however, hit a small boy who was lame. The agonized mother ran to his rescue, but when she picked up the boy, there were no marks of injury or bleeding. On the contrary, the lameness was gone and the boy could walk normally. In another case, a stone hit a young girl, who moved about naked, being of unsound mind. The stone hit her on the forehead. Her mother ran to her rescue, but the girl ran past her and disappeared in the house and hurriedly put on a saree to cover her nakedness. Gone was her madness or dumbness. She became normal. The crowd witnessed these miracles and fell prostrate at the *faqir's* feet and sought His blessings.

Baba's second Visit to Shirdi

After staying at Dhoopkheda for a few says, the young *fakir* (Baba) accepted the request of Chand Bhai Patil to accompany Him and the marriage party of Chand Bhai's nephew Hamid (son of his younger brother Amin Bhai) who was to be married to Chand Bhai's niece at Shirdi. The marriage party reached Shirdi in bullock carts. The bullock carts halted outside Shirdi, near Khandoba Temple. When the young *faqir* got down from the bullock cart, Mlahaspati recognized him and addressed him spontaneously with joy, *"Ya Sai"* (Welcome Sai). While the marriage party went to the bride's house, Baba stayed with Mlahaspati for some time. There is the story of how Baba accepted this name 'Sai' given by Mlahaspati. Baba told Mlahaspati that He would accept this new name 'Sai' after few days. When the marriage was over and Chand Bhai and his party were to return to Dhoop Kheda, he requested Baba to accompany them but Baba told him that He would henceforth stay there at Shirdi.

After a few days, Baba called Mlahaspati and some villagers and asked them to dig the ground under the *neem* tree where He used to stay during His earlier visit to Shirdi – the spot which He used to call *Gurusthan* of the *Guru* of one of His previous lives. He said, "If after digging the land there, four earthen candles would be found in the ground, I would accept the name 'Sai' forever." This actually happened on digging and so He gladly accepted this name and from that day onwards He was called "Sai Baba" or *'faqir Sai'* by all the villagers.

On the day of His arrival at Shirdi, He was dressed in a long, loose white *kurta*, and a green coloured *Kafni* (head-dress) and over it a *bhagvi* (ochre coloured cap). He had a small *danda* (baton) and a *chilam* (clay pipe) in one handand He carried the 'brick' in a cloth in the form of a *potli* (bag) hanging on His other shoulder.

Mlahaspati respected Him, but considering Him to be a Muslim did not allow Him to stay in the Khandoba Temple or his own house in the village. For a few days, the father-in-law of Hamid (who was perhaps named as Amin Bhai of Shirdi) fed Baba while He chose to stay at His old place, the *neem* (margosa) tree of His Gurusthan. Once there were heavy rains which caused a sort of flood. Water and dirt of the village flowed over the body of Sai Baba who was half reclining in the stateof *Samadhi*. Mlahaspati and other villagers were pained to see Him in such a condition. They persuaded Him not to stay there in the open any longer but to stay in an old, dilapidated, mud-built and long forsaken mosque outside Shirdi, quite close to the *Gurusthan*. Thus, He shifted to the old mosque which He named as *'Dwarka Mai Masjid'*.

Ramgir Bua was a boy of 8-9 years of age studying in the village primary school when Baba had come to stay in *Dwarka Mai Masjid* in 1858. In his memoirs of Sri Sai Baba of those days, he writes:

"When Baba came (to Shirdi), He had long hair flowing down to His buttocks. He wore a green skull cap over his hair and over it a *bhagawi* (ochre colored) *topi* with a *chilam* and matchbox...he got his bread by begging. Yamunabai's mother-in-law (teli Narayan's wife), next door to the mosque used to give him a *roti*.

Tatya Baba Kote informs us that before coming to stay in the *masjid*, village children used to pelt stones at Baba thinking Him to be a mad *fakir* since He used to live for some time in the jungle of thorny *babul* trees near Gurusthan.

Shama, who was the school teacher in the Government Primary School, which adjoined the Dwarka Mai Masjid, recalls:

"I was an Assistant Teacher in a school which was located in the place where Baba's horse in now stabled. A window of that always looked on the adjoining mosque. Through that I occasionally watched Baba who was taken by people to be a mad *faqir*. I had no regard for Him then…I used to sleep in the school. Baba was the sole occupant of the mosque, yet I could hear English, Hindi and many other languages being spoken in the mosque (at night) evidently by Baba. I inferred that he had remarkable powers and began to have faith in Him.

It appears that because of this, Baba one day went to the nearby village of Rahata, met Khulshal Chand Sait (Seth) there who suggested to Him to stay in one of the mosques in Rahata permanently. But after a few days of stay at Rahata, during which Kushal Chand served Him with love and reverence, Baba decided to return to Shirdi and stay in Dwarka Mai *Masjid* permanently on the pursuation of a delegation of the devellers of Shirdi.

He used to beg for food two, three times and on some days, even more. He used to beg at the houses of only five persons. Gradually, the villagers of Shirdi developed love and reverence for Him as He started acting as a village *hakim* (physician) who used to give very unconventional medicines as a cure for diseases.

Baba started curing those who cared to ask Him for any miraculous and immediate cure of their physical ailments. He would give crushed leaves, mostly of *Surajmukhi* or anything He could lay His hands on to the patients and these cured wonderfully. Sometimes He used to prepare a *Kadha* (boiled mixture) of *sonamukhi* and some other indigenous medicines and gave one cup full of it everyone present in His Masjid once a month for good health. Sai Sharnananda has mentioned:

At the start, Sai Baba prescribed and gave medicines but never charged any money for the same. Not only that but if He found that there was none to look after or nurse His patient, He would Himself be his nurse and serve him.

Once it so happened that His patient failed to observe the rules of diet, etc., that He had prescribed and as a result thereof he died. Since that day Baba gave up administering medicines and gave only His *udi* (holy ash) for relief.

About the patient who died, we learn from his cousin, Raghuji Ganapati Shinde Patel:

"As soon as Baba came to Shirdi, one Amin Bhai, a Muslim, gave Him food. That Amin Bhai was visiting my *mausi's* (mother's sister) house occasionally. Her son, Ganapati Hari Kanade, aged 35, had leprosy and fever. Amin Bhai told her that a holy man had come to his house and that He could treat her son. Then Baba came to his house and saw the patient. He told Ganapati to catch a cobra courageously as the cobra would not bite a leper. Ganapati caught a cobra and out of its poison, the medicine was prepared and given to Ganapati. He began to improve in few days, but he did not observe Baba's injunctions to avoid sexual pleasures, so Baba stopped giving him further treatment. The disease developed and Ganapati died."

Although Baba gave up practicing as a *hakim* after this incident, He did give *udi* and also other things like groundnuts, grams, sweets, etc., to his devoted patients throughout His life. It may be mentioned that at that time in Shirdi there lived a *vaidya* (local doctor) who was alarmed by Baba's curing the villagers with His free and instantly effective unconventional cures, and fearing that his reputation and income as a *vaidya* would go down for many years to rest, he would constantly oppose Baba and instigate the villagers against him.

Events from 1858 to 1891

From 1858 to 1891, i.e., for 33 years till Baba turned 53, His name and fame was, by and large, confined to Shirdi and the nearby villages of Rahata and Neemgaon; very few devotees from other places came to Him. There might have been many events in those years, but there are no documentary evidences now available about them. The notable incidents during this period of 33 years were:

Baba established *dhooni* (fireplace) in His Dwarka Mai Masjid around 1858 by burning the wood with the flame of the sacred lamp of His *Gurusthan* or maybe, by miraculous materialization of fire.

Baba's Masjid was renovated by His ardent devotees like Mlahaspati and others and the practice of plastering it with cowdung and decorating it started.

Baba developed asthma around the age of 45 and in 1855 had an acute attack, Baba left His physical body for three days entrusting it to the care of Mlahaspati. The villagers and government officials started seriously thinking of disposing of the dead body after two days but Mlahaspati resisted their efforts saying that Baba's life would indeed return to the body after 72 hours and this actually happened.

33

One Muslim magician and wrestler Moinuddin challenged Baba (who also sometimes did wrestling with some of the villagers) to a wrestling bout. Baba accepted the challenge, but was defeated. Thereafter, He started covering His head and moved to the nearby jungle for some months and returned to the *Masjid* afterwards.

In 1890, one elderly Muslim saint, Javar Ali, came to Shirdi; he stayed with Baba and started treating Baba as his disciple. He forced Baba to accompany him to Rahata; they stayed there in a moque for some weeks; the villagers of Shirdi led by Mlahaspati went in deputation to Him and forced Him by their requests to return to Shirdi. Then as Javar Ali was humiliated by Saint Jankidas in spiritual contest, he fled away from Shirdi leaving Baba at *Dwarka Mai*.

Events from 1891 to 1918

The name and fame of Sai Baba spread like wildfire in the nearby villages and tehn to the neighbouring states or regions soon after 1892 when He performed the miracle of lighting the lamps of Dwarka Mai Masjid only with water, after shopkeepers refused to give Him oil on Diwali day.

From 1896, Baba started the annual *Ram Navami-Urs Utasava* (celebrations) in order to forge Hindu-Muslim unity in Shirdi and infuse human values and spirituality among all people who participated in these celebrations.

During 1892-1918, He performed many astounding miracles. Many saints and their disciples came to Shirdi to receive Baba's blessings. Countless people of all religions, castes and social standing came to seek Baba's grace protection and miraculous cures and spiritual enlightenment.

The most widely talked about miracles were: Jamner incident in 1904 in which Baba materialized the horse carriage with its horse, driver and attendant (to carry Ramgir Bua) which had been sent by Baba to deliver His *udi* and *arti* to relieve Mina Tai, daughter of Nana Saheb Chadorkar, who was having a difficult delivery; saving the villagers of Shirdi from plague in 1910; and Baba's assumption of the form of the three-headed divine child Dattatreya on the Dattatreya *Jayanti* in 1911.

Baba's Habits

Many interesting things are now known about Baba's habits. He very carefully and delicately washed His hands and feet before lunch. He took His bath, mostly at the well located Lendi Bagh, then a somewhat far off *jungle*. He did not clean His teeth with any twig, brush, powder, toothpaste or salt.

He was fond of smoking His *chillum* and although many of His devotees presented him a number of such *chillums*, He just stored them but used His own old *chillum*. Many of these chillums are still preserved in the Sri Shirdi Sai Sansthan. Baba also used to allow His devotees to share His *chillum*.

Baba sometimes used to stitch His tattered clothes with needle and thread in the mosque when alone. In the early years, one devotee, Balaji Shimpi, used to give a pair of dress to Baba once a year, but later on he developed an ego and so His economic condition fast deteriorated because of it. Baba did not accept any money for His medical cures but He Himself asked for *dakshina* (cash offering) of modest amounts, like one rupee or even less to anything up to Rs.200/- or evenmore, at a time, repeatedly from His favourite devotees and visitors on whom He wanted to shower His grace, or whom He wanted to protect by teaching a lesson of ego-destruction.

Baba used to abuse and even sometimes beat His devotees in anger. It has been said that His abuses were really directed towards the evil forces, obstacles, diseases or misfortunes of the devotees concerned, not towards the people as such. Mama Dube, a contemporary devotee of Baba, recalled this experience in 1912:

"...I went to the gate of the mosque. Baba was in a towering passion, fuming and fretting with a stone in His hand and was moving up and down the mosque. He saw me standing at the gate. In ten minutes time, He calmed down and took His seat on the *gadi* (seat cushion). That was the place where He should be approached and I went and prostrated. Of his own accord. He said, Take udi and go away. Lakshman Bhatt Joshi of Shirdi recalled:

"As I was quite a boy when I was with Sai Baba, my thoughts were not serious and I cannot repeat the talks He gave. I would run about doing miscellaneous work at the mosque and odd jobs for Radhakrishna Ayi. Madhava Fasli did the same. We would sleep with Baba in the Chawdi. We were allowed to be with Him when none else were allowed. "*Bhai*(brother), carry that log of fuel here. *Bhai*, bring that tub of water, etc." Baba would tell us many things. I would be feasted on the perpetual flow of edibles that would be presented to and then distributed by Baba. He would have basketful of fruits often and we would occasionally purloin some. Baba would sometimes see us and humorously say, "Do not take too much". Often He would abuse me. Once or twice He beat me with His hands. He would occasionally send for me at night, at Chawdi, and ask me to sing, "Sing Ganu's songs or *tukadas*." I would joke by singing songs in His praise lightheartedly. *'Rahama Najar karo ab morey Sai'*, etc. Baba would occasionally Himself get into elated spirits and then (when no one else was present) at dead of the night would sing songs Himself, sometimes Kabir's songs, etc. I do not remember anything now of what He sang."

Sri Shirdi Sai Babas's Lifestyle
Daily Routine

Baba got up very early and sat by His *dhuni* (fireplace). After He finished answering nature's call, he sat quietly for a while. In the meanwhile, Bhagoji Scinde, a leper, came there and undoing the bandages wound around Baba's right hand massaged the hands and the whole body. Then he prepared the *chillum* and gave it to Sai Baba who smoked it, and gave it to Bhagoji for smoking. After the *chillum* had passed hand to hand five or six times, Bhagoji left.

Then Baba got up to wash His mouth and face. He poured a lot of water on hands, feet, mouth, ears and cleaned all parts of His body in a delicate manner. He followed the same process while taking His bath. After washing His mouth, He went out for *bhiksha* (begging alms) to the five fixed place. He would stand in front of the houses of the following blessed persons, begging for alms, in these words:

Nandu Ram Marwadi's House: *"Hey Nandu Ram, bhakari de."* (O, Nandu Ram, give me bread.)

Tatya Patil Kote's House: *"Hey Bayja maa, jevan aan."* (O, Bayja mother, bring me meals

Apaji Kote Patil's house: *"Hey Appa, bhakari de."* (O Appa, give Me bread.)

Vamanrao Gondkar's House: *"Vamanrao, bhakari aan."* (Vaman, bring Me bread.)

Whatever food was offered to Him, He would keep the bread and dry foods in the fold of the cloth hanging over His shoulder, and all liquid foods like dal, vegetable soups, curds, etc. He received in a tin pot (tamrol) held in His hand. He brought the food to the mosque, put all of it in the earthen plate, mixed it and kept it in the open. Birds, squirrels and dogs took a part of it freely. Baba took some of it and the rest of it was distributed to the devotees. Many devotees brought *thalis* full of various kind of delicacies as well as simple food like *roti, rice, khichri, pulao*, etc., for Him, but He merely touched and returned them as His *prasad* (consecrated food), accepting only part of it sometimes, most of which He distributed then and there to the devotees present. One bread was daily sent by Him as *prasad* to Radha Krishna Ayi, His great devotee.

After this *'chotta hazri'* (early light breakfast), Baba held a *darbar* (audience) at which most of His devotees and visitors assembled. Baba gave them advice through direct words of instruction, admonitions or through stories and parables. At times, Baba purchased fruits and distributed them among those present, serving some of them with His own hands.

After this *durbar*, Baba went to Landi, a nearby garden. There He stayed for about an hour. After returning from Landi, Baba stayed in the Masjid till 2 p.m. during which interval He allowed Himself to be worshipped by His devotees through individual *pujas* and then a general or common *aarti*.

Then He had His lunch. At that time, a cloth curtain was drawn in the *masjid* and Baba sat behind it and ate. No one was allowed to enter the mosque at that time, or to peep behind the curtain. Again Baba went to Lendi after about three-quarters of an hour. Then He came to the *Masjid* and sat there till sunset when he went out for some time and was again seated in the *Masjid*. As a rule, there were three general or common sittings or *durbar* during the day – the first one in the morning after breakfast, the second after Baba's return from Lendi, and the third at about 5 p.m.

Baba's contemporary devotees and close workers, like Abdul, have left behind valuable bits of information about Baba's daily routine and habits. Abdul recalled:

Baba sat behind what is now a pillar-like structure at the Lendi which a 'Nanda Deepam' or perpetually burning lamp is kept. I generally found that Baba sat behind the Lendi pillar which enclosed the lamp and not in front of it. From there the lamp was not visible to Him. I never saw Him gazing at the lamp. I used to fill two pots with water and place them near Baba at the Lendi lamp place. He would sit near two such potsfull of water, and He would go on pouring water in various directions. What that was for and whether He would utter any mantra while doing so, I cannot say. Other than me, no one else was present when He poured out water as stated above.

Mrs. Manager, a devotee from Bomay/ recalls:

"He would sit in the mornings near His *dhuni* (fire) and wave His arms and fingers about, making gestures which conveyed no meaning to us, saying, *"Haq"*, i.e., God. Purity, strength, regularly and self-denial one always noticed about Him. He would always beg His food. Even during His illness, He never lay bedridden but would get up and go around to beg His food."

Raghuvir B. Purandhare recalls:

"Baba used to be near the *dhuni*, early morning facing south, leaning on a post and doing something. I cannot say what. People were not allowed to go near, not even 50 feet. The *sevakar* could carry on their usual service or work of clearing or replenishing *dhuni*, etc. no one else could go so near as they. He used to utter words like *'Yade Haq'*. They were seldom clear or audible to us at some distance. *'Allah Malik, Allah Vali hai'*, i.e., God is the Master and Protector, He used to say this at all times.

Das Ganu Maharaj testifies: "Baba did not say His five *namaz* or even one *namaz* as Muslims do. When *fatia* had to be done he generally ordered it to be pronounced by someone present. Sometimes He uttered *fatia*. He occasionally used to repeat parts of the *Quran.*"".

Abdul Rahim Samsuddin Rangari recalls his visit to Baba in 1913:

"I found Baba was smeared with sandal paste over His hand, face, etc. Moslems do not smear themselves like this. I asked Him how He put on all this. Baba said *"Jaisa desh, taisa vesh"*. (Do as the Romans do). Instead of worshipping their Gods, they worship Me as their God. Why should I object and displease them? I am myself a devotee of God.

Bayyaji Apaji Patel recalls:

"I knew Baba since my boyhood. My house was one of the few houses from which Baba took His *bhiksha*, i.e., begged for His bread from the beginning of His life here and upto the end. For some 3 years, Baba would go about 8 times during the day to our house to beg for His bread. Next, for 3 years He visited us for this purpose four times a day. For 12 years He came to us for bread once a day only. From my 11 years onwards, I used to serve Baba. In 1986, i.e., my 7 years, the *Ram Navmi Urs* celebrations began. It was then that Baba allowed Hindus to offer to do *pooja* to Him and Moslems to read *Quran* before Him at the *Masjid*...When Hindus affixed sandal paste to Baba, the latter applied *sandal* marks with the hands (*panja* marks) on the walls of the *Masjid* and other Muslims did the same. Moslems and Mlahaspati in turn applied it to Baba's forehead. Baba then allowed *namaz* to go on at the mosque and enjoined silence on all others while *namaz* was going on. Baba Himself recited the *namaz* sometimes and that was only on Saturdays, when *pedas* or other sweets were brought to Baba, He uttered the *Kalama* (which is the same as *Fatwa*) over the sweets and then distributed them to all – Hindus and Muslims alike."

Bapu Rao N. Chandorkar states:

"All *mantras* that Baba spoke or recited were Arabic or Persian, and not Sanskrit, so far as I know. Kondaji and Bbaa recited *fatwas*. When *'sera'* was brought by people for placing it on the *niche (Kaaba)*, Baba and Kondaji placed it repeating something in Arabic, Persian or some such language."

China Krishna Raja Saheb Bahadur testified as under:

"Baba really cared nothing for money or for presents. What He really wanted was deep love..."

Prof. Narke found that: "He kept women at a distance. During the day, a very few women were allowed to massage His legs and that only up to the knee. He was always properly clad and never indecently exposed Himself."

According to Mrs. Manager:

"He was always in the all-knowing state. Sai Baba was one whom some people would not understand at all. He would talk to a hawker about some cloth brought for making *kafnis*, higgle like the most priser shopper at a bazaar and bring down the price of the cloth, say from 8 annas a yard to 5 annas a yard and take, say 40 yards. By this act the hasty onlooker would conclude that Sai Baba was being parsimonious or at any rate attached to wealth. A little later, He (Sai Baba) would pay the hawker, sometimes ever four times the price settled. Again the hasty onlooker would conclude that Baba was crazy, touched in the brain, or needlessly ostentatious in His misplaced charity. In both cases, the hasty judgments would be wide off the mark and the real reasons for Sai Baba's conduct would remain a mystery to all except those whom He meant to enlighten..

Baba demanded *dakshina* (cash offerings) from many of His devotees and visitors. During the last ten years of His life. He was getting a daily income of Rs. 500 to Rs. 1000 per day which was more than the salary of a British Governor, but He distributed all his daily income from *dakshina* every day in the evening to His close devotees and *faqirs*.In this connection, the following testimonies are pertinent:

Chakranarayana, Police Fauzdar at Kopargaon in October, 1918, recalls:

"Whatever He got, He scattered with a liberal hand. When He died, we took possession of His cash; that was only Rs. 16/-, and yet daily He was paying or giving away hundreds of rupees. Often we noticed that His receipts were smaller than His disbursements. Wherefrom came the excess for Him to disburse or pay, we could not make out.This made me conclude that He had divine powers".

Das Ganu reports:

Several of those that He was regularly paying everyday were subjected to income tax. After Lokamanya Tilak visited Baba (1915-1917) the Income-tax Department directed its attention to the Shirdi Samsthan. Some officer came to Shirdi and watched the income. They first wanted to tax Sai Baba, but (perhaps seeing that He had little left with Him to proceed upon) they taxed His regular donors, viz., Tatya Patel, Bade Baba, Bagua and Bayyaji Patel.

In his renowned Gujarati edition of 'Sri Sai Baba' (1981), Baba's eminent devotee Sai Sharnananda has recorded that Baba used to pay the following amounts in charity daily to the following devotees:

Bade Baba: Rs. 30-55/-	Tatya Patil: Rs. 15-25/-	Choti Amni: Rs. 2/-
Jamil: Rs. 6/-	Dada Kelkar: Rs. 5/-	Bhagi: Rs. 2/-
Sundari: Rs. 2/-	Bayyaji Patel: Rs. 4/-	Laxmi Bai: Rs. 4/-
Other fakirs and poor persons: Rs. 8/-		

It should be recalled that at that time only one rupee silver coins were in circulation, and that one rupee of that period was equal to much more than Rs. 100/- of today.

Abdullah Jan, a young Muslim *fakir* who came to Shirdi from Peshawar side (North-Western Frontier of the undivided India), during Baba's lifetime has left behind these impressions:

"He fed me and other fakirs abundantly and I resolved to stay on and lead an easy life at Shirdi with Him. This was in 1913. . . Baba was surrounded by crowds in His lifetime and it was hard to find room in the mosque on account of these crowds. What a number of dogs used to swarm round Him whereas now there are very few men and hardly any dogs to be seen at the mosque which is (reported in 1936) as a rule deserted. If Baba's splendour was so short-lived and it faded away so quickly, what of me, a poor him?"

For some years till 1910, on certain days, most probably on Thursdays, Baba used to cook *pulao* rice or sweet rice or some other delicacy in the big *handi* (pot) in the Dwarka Mai Masjid. There are some very thrilling accounts of the eyewitnesses. Some of these from *Shri Sai Sat Charita* are reproduced:

"...When He took it into His mind to distribute food to everyone, He made all preparations Himself from the beginning to end. He depended on nobody and troubled none in this matter. First, He went to the bazaar and bought all the things, corn, flour, spices, etc., for cash. He also did the grinding. In the open courtyard of the *Masjid*, He arranged a big hearth, and burning fire underneath, kept a *handi* over it with a proper measure of water. There were two kinds of *handis*, one small and the other big. There former provided food for 50 persons, the latter for 100, sometimes He cooked *mithe chawal* (sweet rice) and at other times pulao with meat. At times, in the boiling *varan* (soup), He let in small balls of thick or flat breads of wheat flour. He pounded the spices on a stone-slab and put the thin pulverize spices into the cooking pot. He took great pains to make the dishes very palatable. He prepared *ambil* by boiling *jawari* flour in water and mixing it with butter milk. With the food, He distributed this ambil to all alike. To see whether the food was properly cooked or not, Baba rolled up the sleeves of His *kafni* and put His bare arms in the boiling cauldron without the least fear and churned the whole mass from side to side, and up and down. There was never any mark of burns on His arm, nor fear on His face.

"When the cooking was over, Baba got the pots in the Masjid and had them duly consecrated by the *moulvi* (Muslim priest). First He sent part of the food as *prasad* to Mlahaspati and Tatya Patil and then He served the remaining contents with His own hands to all the poor and helpless people, to their heart's content. Those who were accustomed to eating meat were given food from the *handi* as *prasad* and those who were not accustomed were not allowed to touch it.

"... The *handi* (cooking) business went on for some time till 1910 and stopped thereafter...Das Ganu spread the fame of Baba by His *kirtans* far and wide in Bombay Presidency...people began to flock to Shirdi and devotees brought with them various articles for presentation and offered various dishes as *naivaidhya* (offerings). The quantity to naivaidhya offered by them was so much that faqirs and paupers could feed themselves to their heart's content and there would still be some surplus."

Dhumal, Pradhan and Shivamma Thayee had witnessed Baba cooking food in the *handi*(big pots) at the *Dwarka Mai Masjid* and they had corroborated the above description in their testimonies. On her first visit, with her husband, her one-year-old son and lady servant, to Shirdi in 1908, Shivamma Thayee had witnessed the Baba's *handi* scene:

"Baba was fond of cooking for His devotees. On my first visit to Shirdi I myself saw Him preparing *ragi* gruel in a big pot in the *Dwarka Mai Masjid*. Wood was burning in the *chullah* and the *ragi* gruel was boiling. Baba pulled up His sleeve and immersed His right hand in the boiling contents of the cooking pot and stirred it many times. We were surprised to see this great miracle of Baba. Evidently, there was no affect of the boiling contents on His hands. Many people besides me and my family witnessed this sort of cooking done by Baba with rapt attention and wonder, repeating Baba's name silently in our hearts. When the cooking was over, Baba Himself distributed the food, His *prasad*, to all devotees, and even to animals and birds who happened to come to the *Masjid* at that time.

Prof. Narke has recalled that in 1914, one day Baba goat a number of *kafnis* prepared and distributed them among His devotees in the presence of Narke, refusing to give one to him saying, "Do not blame Me for not giving you a *kafni*. That fakir (God) has not permitted Me to give you one."

Baba's Behaviour towards His Devotee

Baba treated His devotee with love and concern. He protected them from their misfortunes through His miracles and words of advice. The devotees worshipped Him as God. They loved Him but at the same time were very much afraid of Him. It was customary for devotees to seek His permission before leaving Shirdi, otherwise they suffered many inconveniences or even misfortunes on the return journey. Usually Baba would ask the devotees to wait for a few days or at least for the next day.

Rao Bahadur Dhumal recalls:

"When I craved for leave, Baba said in His characteristic fashion (reminding one of the forms of regal veto) "...The King will consider. i.e., We shall see (what to do) tomorrow. He stopped Me (at Shirdi) for three days."

Baba used to bless His devotees and departing visitors by placing His hand on their heads and pressing it.

Sri Shirdi Sai Baba

Sanyasi Narayan Ashram informs us:

"Baba had a way of touching (with His palm) the head of the devotee who went to Him. His touch did convey certain impulses, forces, ideas, etc. sometimes, He pressed His hand heavily on the head as though he was crushing out some of the lower impulses of the devotee. Sometimes, He tapped; sometimes He made a pass with the palm over the head, etc. Each had its own effect-making remarkable difference in the sensations for feelings of the devotee."

Devotees had started the practice of washing His feet and taking the *pada-tirtha* (holy water) at the time of seeking Baba's permission for their departure from Shirdi. W. Pradhan has recalled how Babu Chandorkar had placed a plate under Baba's feet and pouring water on them collected the water to be used at home. "That was departure in the traditions of Shirdi. Till then only *udi* was allowed to be taken away and *pada-tirtha* was immediately used up at the *aarthi* or at any rate at Shirdi itself. I too took a cue from Babu and carried Baba's *pada-tirtha* home for the use of my mother and others.

Prof. Narke reveals that Baba was living in and operating in other words also besides this and in an invisible body:

"Baba was frequently talking of His travels in an invisible body across distances of soace (and time). In the mornings, sitting near His *dhuni* (fire) with several devotees, He would say to what distant places He went overnight and what He had done. Those who had slept by His side at the *Masjid* or chavadi knew that His physical body was at Shirdi all the night. But His statements were literally true and were occasionally verified and found correct. He had travelled to distant places in an invisible, i.e., spirit form, and rendered help there. Again, He would frequently talk of post-mortem experiences.

A Shirdi Marwadi's boy fell ill and died. People returned from the funeral to the *Masjid* with gloomy faces. Sai Baba then said of that boy, 'He must be nearing the river now, just crossing it.' I felt the reference could only be to *Vaitarn*i (river in Heaven).

In His 80 year long life, Baba wept only twice – when His ardent devotee Megha died on 19 January, 1912, and when Baba's most cherished possession, the 'brick', had broken as its accidently fell from the hand of the servitor, Madho Fasle one morning in early October 1918.

Khaparde has recorded Megha's death in his *Shirdi Diary* in these poignant words:

"Sai Baba came just as the body of Megha was brought out and loudly lamented his death. His voice was so pathetically woeful that it brought tears to every eye. He followed the body up to the bend in the main road near the village and then went His usual way. Megha's body was taken under the *vata* (banyan tree) and consigned to flames there. Sai Baba could be distinctly heard lamenting his death even at that distance and He was seen waving His hand and swaying as if in *Arti* to say goodbye (to the departed soul).'

When the brick, that was given by Guru Venkush, as hs parting gift to the young Baba(Sai Baba), fell from the boy Madho Fasle's hand and broke while he was cleaning the *Masjid*, Baba shed tears, saying:

"It is not the brick that is broken; it is my destiny. It has been my life's companion and I meditated on the self with its help; it is my very life. It has left me today. I shall not survive for long."

Baba's Unconventional Ideas and Unorthodoxy

A deeper probe into the contemporary devotee's experiences enables us to discover that although Baba believed in the sanctity of one's religious beliefs and did not make fun of oor condemn the iconoclast like Kabir (His earlier incarnation), yet He demonstrated the hollowness or futility of many traditional beliefs and practices. For example, Das Ganu and Kusha Bhav have recalled how Baba teased them for observing the food taboo of not eating onions which Baba ate relishingly everyday. Baba did not approve of the Hindus fasting to earn spiritual merits or *punya* and devotee's keenness to get a *Gurumantra* from Him. Shri Sai Sat Charita records the story of Mrs. Radhabai Deshmukh who resorted to fast into death in order to compel Baba to give her a *mantra* Baba addressed her in these poignant words:

"Oh Mother, why are you subjecting yourself to unnecessary tortures and hastening your death? You are really my mother and I am your child. Take pity on Me and hear me…I served him (my *Guru*) long, very long; still he would not blow any *mantra* into my ears. OH mother, My *Guru* never taught me any *mantra*, then how shall I blew any *mantra* in yoru ears? Do not try to get *mantra* or *updesh* from anybody. Take Me as the sole object of your thoughts and actions and you will, no doubt attain *paramartha*, the spiritual goal of your life.

Baba did not believe in the traditional concepts of pollution. He asked sweets for *naivadhya* to be bought from a *halwai's*(confectioner's) house even when the wife of the confectioner had died of plague in Shirdi on that day and her dead body was lying there. He distributed the sweets so bought from there among His devotees without the least worry about physical or cultural pollution.

He did not keep lepers away from Him. Bhagoji, a leper, was His close devotee who bandaged the burns on His right arm and massaged His body daily for many years, and Baba even shared His *chillum* (Clay pipe) with him."

Mrs. Manager has recalled another very thrilling incident relating to a leper from whom Baba accepted *pedha* (milk sweets) and distributed it among the devotees and ate a part of it Himself as well:

"On one occasion, as I was seated at a short distance from Sai Baba, there came a leper to the mosque. His disease was far advanced. He was stinking and had little strength left in him so that it was with much difficulty and very slowly, he clambered up the three steps of the mosque, moved on the *dhuni* and I, feeling the stench from him intensely, hoped he would clear off. At last when he got down slowly carrying a small parcel wrapped in a dirty cloth, I felt relief and said unto myself, Thank God, he is off.

Sai Baba at once darted a piercing glance at me, and I knew that He had read my thoughts. Before the leper had gone far, Sai Baba called out and sent someone to fetch him back. The man came. It was again the slow process of his clambering up, emitting foul stench all the time; and as the man bowed to Baba, Baba picked up that parcel, saying "What is this?" and opened it. It contained some *pedhas* and Sai Baba took a piece and of all the people present gave it to me only and asked me to eat it. What a horror to eat a thing brought by the stinking leper. But it was Sai Baba's order, and there was no option but to obey. So I ate it up. Sai Baba took another piece and Himself swallowed it and then sent the man away with the remainder. Why he was recalled and I alone became the chosen recipient of His pedha none then understood but I knew fully well that Sai Baba had read my heart and was teaching me a valuable lesson in humility, fraternity, endurance and trust in His Supreme wisdom rather than in my own notions of hygiene and sanitation for safety from disease."

Baba taught a dowry-hungry person a lesson. He did not differentiate between rich and poor, Hindus, Muslims or others. His *durbar* (court) was open to all. All sorts of people came to Him to show their skills and offer their regards and receive His blessings, charities and protection.

The author of *Shri Sai Sat Charita* recalls:

'In the *durbar* of Sri Sai, many personalities appear and play their part, astrologers come and give out their predictions; princess, noblemen, ordinary and poor men, *sanyasis*, *yogis*, singers and others come for *darshan*. Even *mahar* comes and making a *johar* (his salutation) says that Sai is the *mai baap* (parent) who will do away with our rounds of births and deaths. So many others, such as jugglers, *gondhalis*, the blind and the lame, *Nathpanthis*, dancers and other players come and are given suitable reception. Bidding his own time, the *Vanjari* also appeared and played the part assigned to him.

Baba's personality had the essential element of humour also. We come across some interesting examples of His humour. Often He would put on the turban of one of His close devotees and mimic the manner of his walking. Once He pinched His devotee Shama's cheeks with love out of humour. Another time, He described His illness in a humorous language to Khaparde. Baba humorously called Abdul by the nickname of 'My *kava*' (crow). Once Haridwar Bua had a strange experience at Shirdi. Imambhai Chote Khan reported this:

A sparrow used to sit on His head as He went until He dipped for His bath at the stream at the village border. Then, it would go up and sit on a tree and resume its seat on His head after the bath was over. We saw this. In our presence, Haridwar Bua asked Baba what this phenomenon signified. Baba said, "*La ilaha illilha. Kya bada durbar hai. munshiji to andha hai. Sardarji c....a hai. Allah malik hai. Allah achcha karega.*" (God is great. What a great *durbar* it is. The minister is blind, the Chief Minister is a fool. God alone is the Master. He will set things right.)

Once while massaging Baba's body, the faces of two devotees an old man and an old lady touched, and the lady humorously complained to Baba that He wanted to kiss her. Baba enjoyed the humor and commented, "what harm is there in kissing one's mother?"

In order to accomplish a grand *avataric* role, He adopted certain distinguishing role-functioning styles of His own, which included the following:

(i) *Setting before people His Ideal life model*

All the testimonies presented above unmistakably establish that Sai Baba had an impeccable character. He had no attraction for wealth, women, grandeur, publicity or influence. He had no likes and dislikes of His own. He had no enemies, no family institution or favourites to worry about. He was truly a model of Brahamjnani, and His life was a unique demonstration lesson of "Simple Living and High Thinking" and "Secular in Practice" to all learners from diverse socio-cultural and economic backgrounds. He taught mainly through the example of moral and spiritual life that He Himself led. The charm or charisma of His total personality influenced most of the people.

(ii) *Using miracles to cure and guide people*

Sai Baba employed His remarkable powers to read people's mind instantly, to immediately know the diverse happenings of the past, present and future, far or near – in every case, to provide miraculous cures, protection and help to most of His devotees and visitors, and to reform people and help them in their spiritual elevation. He had tremendous control over the forces of nature and the destinies of all creatures. He occasionally demonstrated His powers to protect, guide and help His devotees. Although He could do any miracle, it was not in His role-functioning style to do the miracles of materializing *vibhuti, kumkum, haldi, amrit, honey, shivlinga*, lockets, rings, watches, ornaments, pictures, medicines, diamonds, etc., and leaving them behind at the devotees houses as His visiting cards as is the role-functioning style of Sri Sathya Sai Baba today. Sri Shirdi Sai Baba did not need to do such miracles of 'Visiting Cards' as most of the illiterate or even less educated people in those days were simple-hearted and pious people having a great deal of faith and veneration for the divinity.

(iii) *Baba's appearance in devotees' dreams*

'Devotees Experiences of Sai Baba' and other books on Him are full of examples in which Baba appeared in the dreams of many of His devotees to guide, correct, instruct or bless them. This was His most popular role-functioning style as a divine personality, and He continues to do so.

(iv) *Baba's anger*

Baba often showed His anger by abusing some people and also beating sometimes, but evidence confirms the popular belief in the devotees that all His anger, abuses, beating, etc., were in fact directed towards the evil spirits, misfortunes, evil planets, or obstacles in the lives of His devotees or earnest visitors. So they had their inner meanings. On the physical plane, however, they were instruments to discipline, socialize, reform or correct people in the same way as a loving mother or a teacher sometimes beats or shows anger towards a naughty child.

(v) *Baba's humor*

Baba's humor was also one of His role-functioning styles which brought him closer to the hearts of His devotees, relieved them of the atmosphere of tension caused by the fear of Baba's towering personality and created moments of joy, which the participants long cherished.

(vi) *Baba's emphasis on religious co-existence*

The testimonies of many devotes clearly indicate that Baba's role-functioning style was characterized by a spirit and an earnest effort to live the ideal of religious coexistence – secularism par excellence. He was born a Hindu, brought up by a Muslim *faqir* family and a Hindu *Guru* and He allowed both Hindu and Muslim devotees to pray to Him as Eeswara or Allah, encouraging both sets of religious beliefs and modes of worship in His Mosque to which He gave the Hindu name *'Dwarka Mai'*.

Nowhere in the world, in any age, can one find a parallel of such a thrilling, matchless and genuine example of divine role-paying as a promoter of religious co-existence and of genuine, simple and pure spirituality. There was no artificially or element of show-worship or deception in it as is the style of many of the modern *Gurus, Acharayas* and Godly personalities with their politically supporting patrons and followers.

(vii) *Baba's role-functioning style – a Modified Form of Kabir's style*

It is interesting to learn from Baba that He was Kabir in one of His previous births. In both these births, as Kabir and as Sai Baba of Shirdi, the role-sets and the concerns of the two avatars were essentially the same – to promote *bhakti* (devotion) of the God in the masses, to make them understand the shallowness or hypocrisy of their fundamentalist stands and diehard rituals and to make them honest, pious, egoless and dedicated beings, who preferred not to become *vanprasthis* (forest dwellers) and sanyasis seeking spiritually elevation, but who instead stayed in society, performing their worldly duties in a detached manner, serving humanity and yet rising higher and higher in their spiritual search, not through *dhyana* or yoga But by their simple acts of piety, kindness and service to all creatures who had full realization of fundamental spiritual truth that all them had the same soul, all felt hungry and thirsty, all suffered pain and misery and therefore all deserved equal respect and help.

Kabir in his role-functioning style was an iconoclast – a ruthless social critic, and a fiery crusading social activist who waged a *jehad* against the *Pandits, Mullahs, Mandirs, Masjid, Kaba* and *Kashi*, and all sorts of belief and practices of the Hindus and Muslims, to purge their minds of all germs of irrationality, hypocrisy, religious harsonien and fundamentalism. On the other hand, during His reincarnation in the 19th-20th centuries, Sri Sai Baba chose to play a positive, appreciative, integrative or conjunctive social interactionist role. He allowed the Hindus as well as the Muslims to continue following their own religious and spiritual beliefs and practices, encouraging the reading of Hindu scriptures (*Gita, Vishnu Sahasranama, Yog Vashishtha, Jnaneswari*, etc.) as well as the *Quran*. Instead of decrying the *Sakar* (formful) gods He demonstrated that they too were as true as the *Nirakar* (formless) God, and that there was only one God and He Himself was that God which was present before all the people at Shirdi.

Thus Sai Baba of Shirdi was in two ways more advanced than Kabir in His role-functioning styles – one, instead of hurting the traditional sentiments. He won the appreciation, love, cooperation, veneration and following of both the communities; and two, He won the gratitude and love of all His devotees and visitors by showering His miraculous blessing in the form of cures, removal of impediments and bestowal of good luck; this Kabir did not do.

What Kabir could not accomplish through hundreds of *sakhis, banis, ramanis,* and *padas* full of spirituality and scathing social criticism, Shirdi Sai Baba accomplished with a very few words of positive and intergrative teachings and a few parables and real life stories of the previous births of some creatures. Instead of threatening to shake up and demolish their ancient or traditional beliefs Baba rightly chose to fortify those structures by His love and understanding and then build the edifice of spirituality on them by teaching only the common and most fundamental spiritual truth.

Shirdi Sai Baba's role-functioning style was certainly different from all other previous incarnations of God – many of whom were rulers and warriors born and brought up in royal families who spent many years of their lives fighting with and killing the evil-doers, or those who spent years in meditation in forests and then formed their sects with large followings. Shirdi Sai Baba's role did not envision the destructive role of Shiva; it did not end up in the starting of a new sect, cult, religion or a school of spiritual philosophy. He was the *Avatar* of the Kali age who was solely concerned with the promotion of understanding, regard and unity among the followers of all the existence religions and in making everyone conscious that the popular fallacy of the Kali age that "God is dead" was nothing but sacrilegious.

Chapter – 2

Sai Baba of Shirdi (Wikipedia)

Sai Baba was an Indian spiritual master who was and is regarded by his devotees as a saint, *fakir*, and *Sadguru*. He was reversed by both his Hindu and Muslim devotees. It remained uncertain if he was a Hindu or Muslim himself. This, however, was of no consequence to Sai Baba himself.[2] Sai Baba stressed the importance of surrender to the guidance of the *Sadguru* or *Murshid*, (teacher) who, having gone the path to divine consciousness himself, will lead the disciple through the jungle of spiritual training.[3]

Sai Baba is worshipped by people around the world. He had no love for perishable things and his sole concern was self-realization. He taught a moral code of love, forgiveness, helping others, charity, contentment, inner peace, and devotion to God and guru. He gave no distinction based on religion or caste. Sai Baba's teaching combined elements of Hinduism and Islam: he gave the Hindu name *Dwarakamai* to the mosque he lived in,[4] practiced Muslim rituals, taught using words and figures that drew from both traditions, and was buried in Shirdi. One of his well known epigrams, *"Sab Ka Malik Ek"* ("One God governs all"), is associated with Hinduism, Islam and Sufism. He also said, *"Trust in me and your prayer shall be answered"*. He always uttered "Allah Malik" ("God is King").[3]

Background

No verifiable information is available regarding Sai Baba's real name, place or time of birth. When asked about his past, he often gave elusive responses. The name *"Sai"* was given to him upon his arrival at *Shirdi*, a small village in the Indian state of Maharashtra. Mahalsapati, a local temple priest, recognized him as a Muslim saint and greeted him with the words *'Ya Sai'*, meaning 'Welcome Sai'.

Sai or *Sayi* is a Persian title given to Sufi saints, meaning 'ooor one'[5] The honorific "Baba" means 'father, grandfather; old man, sir" in most Indian and Middle Eastern languages. Thus Sai Baba denotes "holy father", 'saintly father" or "poor old man".[2] Alternatively, the Sindhi and Urdu word "sain" (*), an huonorific title for a virtuoso, a saint, or a feudal lord (i.e. a patron), is derived from the Persian word "sayeh", which literally means 'shadow" but figuratively refers to patronage or protection. The Hindi-Urdu word "Saya" comes from the same borrowing. Thus, it could also mean "Master Father". However, *Sai* may also be an acronym of the Sanskrit item *"Sakshat Eshwar"*, a reference to God. *Sakshat* means "incarnate" and *Eshwar* means "God".

Some of Sai Baba's disciples became famous as spiritual figures and saints, such as Mahalsapati, a priest of the Khandoba temple in Shirdi, and UPasani Maharaj. He was reversed by other saints, such as Saint Bidkar Maharaj, Saint Gangagir, Saint Janakidas Maharaj, and Sati Godavari Mataji. [6, 7] Sai Baba referred to several saints as 'my brothers', especially the disciples of Swami Samartha of Akkalkot.[7]

Early years

Shirdi Sai Baba's biographer Narasimha Swamiji claims that Sai Baba was born as the child of Brahmin parents. "On one occasion, very late in his life, he revealed to Mahalsapathy the interesting fact that his parents were Brahmins of Pathri in the Nizam's State. Pathri is Taluk in Parbhani district, near Manwat. Sai living in a mosque, that while still a tender child his Brahmin parents handed him over to the care of a fakir who brought him up. This is fairly indisputable testimony, as Mahlsapathy was a person of sterling character noted for his integrity, truthfulness and *vairagya*." – Narasimha Swamiji, *Life of Sai Baba*.[8]

According to the book *Shri Sai Satcharita*, Sai Baba arrived at the village of Shirdi when he was about 16 years old. He led an ascetic life, sitting motionless under a *neem* tree meditating while sitting in an *asana*. The *Shri Sai* 'The people of the village were wonder-struck to see such a young lad practicing hard penance, not minding heat or cold. By day he associated with no one, by night he was afraid of nobody'.[9]

His presence attracted the curiosity of the villagers, and he was regularly visited by the religiously inclined, including Mahalsapati, Appa Jogle and

Kashinath. Some considered him mad and threw stones at him.[10] Sai Baba left the villag, and little is known about him after that.

There are some indications that he met with many saints and fakirs, and worked as a weaver. He claimed to have been with the army of Rani Lakshmibai of Jhansi during the first war of Independence 1857.[11] It is generally accepted that Sai Baba returned to Shirdi permanently around 1858, which suggests a birth year of 1838.[12] Around this time he adopted his famous style of dress consisting of a knee-length one-piece *Kafni* robe and a cloth cap. Ramgir Bua, a devotee, testified that Sai Baba was dressed like an athlete and sported 'long hair flowing down to the end of his spine' when he arrived in Shirdii, and that he never had his head shaved. It was only after Baba forfeited a wresting match with one Mohiddin Tamboli to Baba's identification as a Muslim fakir and was a reason for initial indifference and hostility against him in a predominantly Hindu village.[14]

During his first visit to and stay at Shirdi he used to live under q *neem* tree and often wandered for long periods in the jungle around Shirdi. His manner was said to be withdrawn and uncommunicative as he undertook long periods of meditation.[15] On his second coming to Shirdi He was eventually persuaded to take up residence in an old and dilapidated mosque and lived a solitary life there, surviving by beginning for alms, and receiving itinerant Hindu or Muslim visitors. In the mosque he maintained a sacred fire which is referred to as dhuni, from which he gave sacred *'Udhi'* (ashes) to all people and visitors before they left. The *Udi* was believed to have healing powers. He performed the function of a local *hakim* (healer) by freely treating the sick by application of ashes and unusual prescriptions.

Sai Baba also delivered spiritual teachings to his visitors, recommending the reading of sacred Hindu texts along with the *Quran*. He insisted on the indispensability of the unbroken remembrance of God's name *(dhikr, japa)*, and often expressed himself in a cryptic manner with the use of parables, symbols and allegories.[16]

After 1910 Sai Baba's fame began to spread in Mumbai. Numerous people started him, because they regarded him as a saint with the power of performing miracles or even as an *Avatar* (incarnation of God).[17] They built his first temple at Bhivpuri, Karjat.[18]

Teachings and practices

Sai Baba opposed all persecution based on religion or caste. He was an opponent of religious orthodoxy – Christian, Hindu and Muslim.[19] He encouraged his devotees to pray, chant God's name, and read holy scriptures. He told Muslims to study the Quran and Hindus to study texts such as the Ramayana, Bhagavad Gita and *Yoga Vasistha*.[20] He was impressed by the philosophy of the *Bhagavad Gita* and encouraged people to follow it in their own lives.[21] He advised his devotees and followers to lead a moral life, help others, love every living being without any discrimination, and develop two important features of character: devotion to the Guru *(Sraddha)* and waiting cheerfully with patience and love *(Saburi)*. He criticized atheism.[22]

In his teachings, Sai Baba emphasized the importance of performing one's duties without attachment to earthly matters and of being content regardless of the situation. In his personal practice, Sai Baba observed worship procedures belonging to Hinduism and Islam; he shunned any kind of regular rituals but allowed the practice of namaz, chanting of *Al-Fatiha*, and Qur'an readings at Muslim festival times.[23] Occasionally reciting the Al-Fatiha himself, Baba enjoyed listening to *mawlid* and *qawwali* accompanied with the *tabla* and *sarangi* twice daily.[24]

Sai Baba interpreted the religious texts of both Islam and Hinduism. He explained the meaning of the Hindu scriptures in the spirit of *Advaita Vedanta*. His philosophy also had numerous elements of bhakti. The three main Hindu spiritual paths – *Bhakti Yoga, Jnana Yoga,* and Karma Yoga – influenced his teachings.[1]

Sai Baba encouraged charity, and stressed the importance of sharing. He said: "Unless there is some relationship or connection, nobody goes anywhere. If any men or creatures come to you, do not discourteously drive them away, but receive them well and treat them with due respect. Shri *Hari* (God) will certainly be pleased if you give water to the thirsty, bread to the hungry, clothes to the naked, and your verandah to strangers for sitting and resting. If anybody wants any money from you and you are not inclined to give, do not give, but do not bark at him like a dog."[25]

Shirdi Sai Baba spiritual movement

The Shirdi Sai Baba movement began in the 19th century, while he was living in Shirdi. The local Khandoba temple priest, Mhalsapati his first devotee. In the 19th century Sai Baba's followers were only a small group of Shirdi inhabitants and a few people from other parts of India! Because of Sai Baba, Shirdi has become a place of importance and is counted among the major Hindu places of pilgrimage!

The Sai Baba Mandir in Shirdi is visited by over 20,000 pilgrims daily and by lakhs on festival days a day and curing religious festivals this number can reach up to a 100,000.[26] Shirdi Sai Baba is especially revered and worshiped in the states of Maharashtra, Odisha, Andhra Pradesh, Karnataka Tamil Nadu and Gujarat. In August 2012, an unidentified devotee for the first time donated two costly diamonds valuing Rs.11.8 million at the Shirdi temple, SaiBaba trust officials revealed.[27]

The Shirdi Sai movement has spread to the Caribbean and to countries such as the Nepal, United States, Australia, United Arab Emirates, Malaysia, United kingdom, Germany, France and Singapore.[28] Recently on *Guru Purnima* festival day the Government of Nive island in Silver Sai Baba coin.

Notable disciples

Sai Baba left behind no spiritual heirs, appointed no disciples, and did not even provide formal initiation (*diksha*), despite requests. Some disciples of Sai Baba achieved fame as spiritual figures, such as Upasni Maharaj of Sakori.

Claimed miracles

Sai Baba's disciples and devotees claim that the performed many miracles such as bi-location, levitation, mindreading, materialization, exorcism, making the river Yamuna, entering a state of *Samadhi* at will, lighting lamps with water, removing his limbs or intestines and sticking them back to his body *(Khandana yoga)*, curing the incurably sick, appearing beaten when another was beaten, preventing a mosque from falling down on people, and helping his devotees in a miraculous way. He also gave *darshan* (vision) to people in the form of Sri Rama, Krishna, Vithoba and many other gods depending on the faith of devotees.[30] According to his followers he appeared to them in dreams and gave them advice and does so even now throughout the world. His devotees have documented his many miracle stories.[31] Many miracles of Sai Baba's are available on the Internet.

Hinduism

During Sai Baba's life, the Hindu saint Anandanath of Yewala declared Sai Baba a spiritual "diamond".[32] Another saint, Gangagir, called him a "jewel". [32] Sri Beedkar Maharaj greatly revered Sai Baba, and in 1873, when he met him he bestowed the title *Jagat Guru* upon him.[33][34] Sai Baba was also greatly respected by Vasudevananda Saraswati (known as Tembye Swami).[35] He was also revered by a group of *Shaivic yogis*, to which he belonged, known as the *Nath-Panchayat*.[36]

According to B.V. Narasimhaswami, a posthumous follower who was widely praised as Sai Baba's "apostle", this attitude was prevalent up to 1954 even among some of his devotees in Shirdi.[37]

Zoroastrianism

Sai Baba was worshiped by prominent Zoroastrian spiritualist Minocher K. Spencer (author of *'How I Found God'* and his cousin Homi C. Spence, and others like Bakshi, Nanabhoy Palkhivala and Homi Bhabha, and has been cited as the Zoroastrians' most popular non-Zoroastrian religious figure.[38]

Meher Baba, who was born into a Zoroastrian family, met Sai Baba once, during World War I, in December 1915. Meher Baba was a youngster named Merwan Sheriar Irani, when he met Sai Baba for a few minutes during one of Sai Baba's processions in Shirdi. In *'Lord Meher'*, the life story of Meher Baba, there are numerous references to Sai Baba.[29] Meher Baba credited his *Avataric* advent to Upasani, Sai Baba, and three other Perfect Masters: Hazrat Babajan, Hazrat Tajuddin Baba, and Narayan Maharaj. He declared Sai Baba to be a *Qutub-e-Irshad* (the highest of the five Qutubs, a "Master of the Universe" in the spiritual hierarchy).[39]

Sacred art and architecture [edit]

There are many Sai Baba temples in India.[40] There are also temples located in U.S.A., U.K. Netherlands, Kenya, Mauritius, Cuba, Canada, Pakistan, Australia, Germany, China, Japan etc.

There is a life-size Italian marble statue of Sai Baba made of marble by a sculptor named Balaji Vasant Talim of Mumbai in the *Samadhi Mandir* in Shirdi where Sai Baba was buried.[42]

Film and television [edit]

Sai Baba has been the subject of several feature films in many languages produced by India's film industry.

Year	Film	Title role	Director	Language	Notes
1955	Shirdi Che Sai Baba	Unknown	Kumarsen	Marathi	Won all India Certificate of Samarth Merit at 3rd National Film Awards
1977	Shirdi Ke Sai Baba	Sudhir Dalvi Bhushan	Ashok V.	Hindi	Also featuring Manoj Kumar, Rajendra Kumar, Hema Malini, Shatrughan Sinha, Sachin, Prem Nath
1986	Sri Shirdi Sai Baba	Vijayachander	K. Vasu	Telugu Dubbed into Hindi as Shirdi Saibaba Sai Baba Ki Kahani, into Mahathyam Tamil as Sri Shirdi Saibaba.	Also featuring Chandra Mohan, Suthi Veerabhadra Rao, Sarath Babu, J.V.Somayajulu, Rama Prabha, Anjali Devi, Raja.
1989	Bhagavan Sai Baba	Sai Prakash	Sai Prakash Brahmavar	Kannada	Also starring Ramkumar, Vijaylakshmi
1993	Sai Baba Fattelal	Yashwant	Babasaheb S.	Marathi	Also featuring Lalita Pawar Dutt
2000	Maya Sai Baba	Unknown	Ramanarayanan	Tamil	Also featuring S.P. Balasubrahmanyam
2000	Sri Sai Sai Mahima	Prakash	Ashok Kumar	Telugu	Also featuring Murali Mohan, Jaya Sudha, P.J. Sharma
2001	Shirdi Sai Baba	Sudhir Dalvi	Deepak Balraj	Hindi	Also featuring Dharmendra, Rohini Hattangadi, Suresh Oberoi

2005	Ishwarya Avatar Sai Baba	Mukul Nag	Ramanand Sagar	Hindi	Composite movie drawn from Sagar's Sai Baba (TV Series)
2010	Malik Ek	Jackie Shroff	Deepak Balraj	Hindi	Also featuring Manoj Vij, Hattangadi, Zarina, Wahab and Anup Jalota as Cas Ganu
2010	Bhagwan Sri Shirdi Sai Baba	Surya Vasishta	Bukkaata Vasu	Kannada	Also featuring Ravindranath, Ravi Bhat Rai, Chandrika Challakere, and others. Aired on Kasturi (TV channel)
2012	Shirdi Sai	Nagarjuna	K. Raghavendra	Telugu	Released on 6 September. Also Featuring Srikanth, Kamalini Mukherjee, Rohini Hattangadi, Sharat Babu, Brahmanandam

References

1. Rigopoulos, Antonio (1993). *The Life and Teachings of Sai Baba of Shirdi.* pp. 261-352. ISBN 0-7914-1268-7.

2. Rigopoulos, Antonio (1993). *The Life and Teachings of Sai Baba of Shirdi.* p. 3. ISBN 0-7914-1268-7-

3. *Shri Sai Satcharitra*

4. Hoiberg, Dale; I. Ramchandani (2000). *Students Britannica India.* Popular Prakashan, 1 December 2007.

5. Rigopoulos, *The Life and Teachings of Sai Baba of Shirdi.*

6. Ruhela, S.P. (ed.), *Truth in Controversies about Sri Shirdi Sai Baba,* Faridabad, Indian Publishers Distributors, 2000. ISBN 81-7341-121-2

7. Dabholkar, Govind Raghunath, *Shri Sai Satcharita: the life and teachings of Shirdi Sai Baba* (1999).

8. Narasimha Swamiji, *Life of Sai Baba,* p.16.

9. Rigopoulos, Antonio (1993). *The Life and teachings of Sai Baba of Shirdi.* SUNY. p. 46. ISBN 0-7914-1268-7.

10. Parthasarathy, Rangaswami (1997). *God Who Walked on Earth: The Life and Times of Shirdi Sai Baba.* Sterling Publishing. p. 15. ISBN 81-207-1809-7.

11. Balakrishna Upasani Shastri, "I was at the battle in which the Rani of Jhansi took part. I was then in the army." Quoted in Narasimhaswami, B.V. (1986). *Sri Sai Baba's Charters & Sayings.* All-India Sai Samaj, Madras, p. 2009.

12. Rigopoulos, Antonio (1993). *The Life and Teachings of Sai Baba of Shirdi..* p. 45. ISBN 0-7914-1268-7.

13. Warren, Marianne (1997). *Unraveling the Enigma: Shirdi Sai Baba in the Light of Sufism.* Sterling Publishers. p. 104. ISBN 81-207-2147-0.

14. Rigopoulos, Antonio. *The Life and Teachings of Sai Baba of Shirdi.* ISBN 0-7914-1268-7.

15. Warren, Marianne (1997). *Unraveling the Enigma: Shirdi Sai Baba in the Light of Sufism.* Sterling Publishers. p. 45. ISBN 81-207-2147-0.

16. Rigopoulos, Antonio (1993). *The Life and Teachings of Sai Baba of Shirdi.* SUNY. p. 86. ISBN 0-7914-1268-7.

17. Warren, Marianne (1997). *Unraveling the Enigma: Shirdi Sai Baba in the Light of Sufism.* Sterling Publishers. pp. 340-341. ISBN 81-207-2147-0.

18. Sai Ananta – Kaka Saheb Dixit Trust of Shri Sai Baba at http://www.saiananta.com

19. Rigopoulos, Antonio (1993). *The Life and Teachings of Sai Baba of Shirdi.* p. 139. ISBN 0-7914-1268-7.

20. Dabholkar/Gunaji *Shri Sai Satcharita/Shri Sai Satcharitra.* Chapter 27.

21. "*Shri Sai Satcharitra*". Sa Baba.org. Retrieved 17 June 2013.

22. Dabholkar/Gunaji *Shri Sai Satcharita/Shri Sai Satcharitra.* Chapter

23. 3 [1].

24. Warren, Marianne (1999). *Unravelling The Enigma: Shirdi Sai Baba in the Light of Sufism.* Sterling Publishers. p. 29. ISBN 0-7914-1268-7.

25. Warren, Marianne (1999). *Unravelling The Enigma: Shirdi Sai Baba in the Light of Sufism.* Sterling Publishers. p. 30. ISBN 0-7914-1268-7.

26. Dabholkar (alias Hemadpant) *Shri Sai Satcharita.* Shri Sai Baba Sansthan Shirdi, (translated from Marathi into English by Nagesh V. Gunaji in 1944) available online or downloadable.

27. "Temple Complex". Archived from the original on 25 October 2007. Retrieved 29 October 2007.

28. "Unknown person donates diamonds worth Rs. 1.18 crore (approximately $240,000) at Shirdi". 1 August 2012.

29. Brady R., Coward H.G., Hinnels J.H. *The South Asian Religious Diaspora in Britain, Canada, and the United States*, p. 93 [2].

30. Sandman (20 January 2009). "Who is Sai Baba guru? Zarzari Zar Baksh who lived at Khuldabad, says Meher Baba". *Asian Tribune*. Retrieved 8 January 2011.

31. Mukund Raj (1 November 2010). "Shri Sai Baba Shirdi Home Page". Saibaba.org. Retrieved 8 January 2011.

32. Ruhela, *Shri Shirdi Sai Baba – the universal master*, pp. 141-154.

33. "Who is Shirdi Sai Baba". Archived from the original on 15 October 2007. Retrieved 29 October 2007.

34. "A Short Biography of Shree Sadguru Beedkar Maharaj". Retrieved 29 October 2007.

35. "Beedkar Maharaj". *Sai Vichaar, Oct. 06, 2005, volume 8, issue 2001*. Retrieved 29 October 2007.

36. Dabholkar/Gunaj, *Shri Sai Satcharita*, chapter 50 [3].

37. Ruhela,S.P., *Shri Shirdi Sai Baba – the universal master*. p. 27.

38. Narasimhaswami, B.V. (1990). *LIfe of Sai Baba (Vol. 1)*. Madras: All-India Sai Samaj. p. 24.: "One very closely associated devotee of his, now living, still believes that Baba was 'only a Mohammadan.' What can 'only a Mohammadan' mean? It means that even after 25 years of personal experience of him and 36 years of his *post mortem* glories, the devotee treats him as a communalist just as he did when Baba was in the flesh." Narasimhaswami, B.V. (1990). *Life of Sai Baba (Vol. 1)*. Madras: All-India Sai Samaj. pp. 24-25.: "Baba wished to convince the devotee, if he was a Hindu, that he was Mahavishnu, Lakshminarayan, etc., and he bade water flow from his feet as Ganga issued from Mahavishnu's feet. The devotee saw it and praised him as '*Rama Vara*', but as for the water coming from his feet, that devotee simply sprinkled a few drops on his head and would not drink it coming as it did from a Mohammadan's feet. So great was the prejudice of ages that even one, who thought of him as Vishnu, thought he was a 'Muslim Vishnu'. Prejudices die hard and the devotee wondered and wonders how people can believe that Baba was a

Brahmin and that his parents were Brahmins when he had lived all his life in a mosque and when he was believed to be a Muslim."

39. Hinnels J.R. *Zoroastrians Diaspora: Religion and Migration.* p. 109.
40. Kalchuri, Bhau: *Meher Prabhu: Lord Meher, The Biography of the Avatar of the Age,* Meher Baba, Manifestation, Inc. 1986. p. 64.
41. Srinivas *Sathya Sai Baba movement.*
42. "Directory of Shri Shirdi Saibaba temples around the world." omsrisai. net Retrieved 17 June 2013.
43. Ruhela.S.P., *Shri Shirdi Sai Baba – The Universal Master.*
44. "Official Page of Bhagwan Sri Shirdi Sai Baba on Facebook".

Further reading

Arulneyam, Durai, *The Gospel of Shri Shirdi Sai Baba. A Holy Spiritual Path,* New Delhi, Sterling, 2008. ISBN 978-81-207-3997-0

1. Babuji, Sri Sainathuni Sarath, 'Arati Sai Baba, *The Psalm Book of Shirdi Aratis, Saipatham Publicaitons, 1996. Available online.*
2. Kamath, M.V. & Kher, V.B., *Sai Baba of Shirdi: A Unique Saint,* India: Jaico Publishing House (1997). ISBN 81-7224-030-9
3. Osborne, Arthur, *The Incredible Sai Baba. The Life and Miracles of a Modern-day Saint,* Hyderabad, Orient Longman, 1957. ISBN 81-250-0084-4
4. Panday, Balkrishna, *Sai Baba's 261 Leelas. A Treasure House of Miracles,* New Delhi, Sterling, 2004. ISBN 81-207-2727-4
5. Parthasarathy, Rangaswami, *God Who Walked on Earth. The Life and Times of Shirdi Sai Baba,* New Delhi, Sterling, 1996. ISBN 81-207-1809-7.
6. Rao, Sham.P.P., *Five Contemporary Gurus in the Shirdi (Sai Baba) Tradition,* Bangalore: Christian Institute for the Study of Religion and Society, 1972. LC Control No.: 75905429
7. Venkataraman, Krishnaswamy, *Shirdi Stories,* Srishti Publishers, New Delhi, 2002. ISBN 81-87075-84-8
8. White, Charles S.J., *The Sai Baba Movement: Approaches to the Study of India Saints* in Journal of Asian Studies, Vol. 31, No. 4 (Aug. 1972), pp. 863-878
9. White Charles S.J., *The Sai Baba Movement: Study of a Unique Contemporary Moral and Spiritual Movement,* New Delhi, Arnold-Heinemann, 1985.

10. Williams, Alison, *Experiencing Sai Baba's Shirdi. A Guide*, revised edition, Shirdi, Saipatham Publications. 2004 ISBN 81-88560-00-6 available online

11. Walshe-Ryan, Lorraine, *I am always with you*, Reprint 2008, New Delhi, Sterling Publishing, 2006. ISBN 978-81-207-3192-9.

12. Guruji Vij Rajesh, Service to Living beings is service to god Jai Sai Naam (1995) India.

Media related to Sai Baba of Shirdi at Wikimedia Commons

Chapter – 3

Sri Shirdi Sai Baba's Teachings and Post-*Samadi* Messages

"If anyone does any evil unto you, do not retaliate. If you can do anything, do something good to others."

-Sri Shirdi Sai Baba

Sri Shirdi Sai Baba was a unique saint in many ways. Although He did not deliver long discourses and did nothing to show Himself as a scholar or a highly learned man, yet whatever little He spoke to teach, guide or spiritualize His devotees, those are indeed unique teachings of the great divine incarnation of this *Kali* age. The particular feature of His teachings was that He could convey the precious contents of His teachings in such forceful, direct, unambiguous few words that even an illiterate person coming from a rural background could very easily understand and assimilate.

Precious Sayings of Sri Shirdi Sai Baba
Action (*Karma*)
This *deha prarabdha* (present fate) is the result of the *karma* (action) done by you in the former births.

Assurance
If a man utters My name with love, I shall fulfil all his wishes and increase his devotion. If he sings earnestly My life and deeds, him I shall be in front and back and on all sides.

Beauty

We have not to bother about beauty or ugliness of the person, but to concentrate solely in God underlying that form.

Charity

The donor gives, that is, sows his seeds, only to reap a rich harvest in future. Wealth should be means to work out *Dharma*. If it is not given before, you do not get it now. So, the best way to receive is to give.

Contentment

One must rest content with one's lot.

Dakshina

The giving of *dakshina* (reverential gift) advances *vairagya* (non-attachment) and thereby *bhakti* (devotion).

• Death

None dies; see with your inner eyes. Then you will realize that you aare God and not different from Him. Like worn out garments the body is cast away,

Disillusion

Whenever any idea of joy or sorrow arises in your mind, resist it. Do not give room to it. It is pure disillusion.

Destiny

Whosoever is destined to be struck will be struck. Whosoever is to die will die. Whosoever is to be caressed will be caressed.

Discrimination

There are two sorts of things – the good and the pleasant. Both these approach man for acceptance. He has to think and choose one of them. The wise man prefers the good to the pleasant but the unwise, through greed and attachment, chooses the pleasant and thereby cannot gain *Brahma gyana* (Self-realization).

Devotee

He who withdraws his heart from wife, child and parents and loves Me is My real lover or devotee and he merges in Me like a river in the sea.

Devotion

Knowledge of the Vedas or fame as a great *jnani* (learned scholar) or formal *bhajan* (religious song) are of no avail unless they are accompanied by *Bhakti* (devotion).

Differences

People differentiate between themselves and others, their properties with other's properties. This is wrong. I am in you and you are in Me. Mediate on the self with a question "Who am I?"

Duty

Unless a man discharges satisfactorily and disinterestedly the duties of his station in his life, his mind will not be purified.

Egoism

The teachings of a *Guru* are of no use to a man who is full of egoism and who always thinks about sense-objects.

Enemy

Who is whose enemy? Do not say of anyone that he is your enemy. All are one and the same.

Equanimity: Let the world go topsy-turvy, you remain where you are. Standing or staying at your own place, look calmly at the show of all things passing before you.

Exploitation

Nobody should take the labor of others *gratis*. The workers should be paid his dues promptly and liberally.

Feeding

Know for certain that he who feeds the hungry, really serves Me with food. Regard this as an axiomatic truth.

Food

Sitting in the *Masjid* (mosque) I shall never, never speak untruth. Take pity on Me like this: first give bread to the hungry and eat yourself. Note this well.

Forbearance

Our *Karma* is the cause of happiness and sorrow. Therefore, put up with whatever comes to you.

God

God lives in all beings and creatures, whether they be serpents or scorpions. He is the greatest wirepuller of the world, and all beings, serpents, scorpion, etc., obey His command.

God's Gifts

What a man gives does not last long and it is always imperfect. But what my *Sircar* (God) gives, lasts to the end of life. No other gift from any man can be compared to His.

God's Grace

You must always adhere to truth and fulfil all the promises you make. Have *shraddha* (faith) and *saburi* (patience). Then I will always be with you wherever you are.

God's Will

Unless God wills it, nobody meets us on the way; unless God wills, nobody can do any harm to others.

Goodness

If you act in a good way, good will really follow.

Greed

Greed and *Brahma* (God) are poles asunder; they are eternally opposed to each other. Where there is greed, there is no room for thought or meditation of the Brahma. Then how can a greedy man get dispassion and salvation?

Guru

Stick to your own Guru with unabated faith, whatever the merits of other gurus and however little the merits of your *Guru* may be.

Guru's Grace

The mother tortoise is on one bank of the river and her younger ones are on the other. She gives neither milk nor warmth to them. Her mere glance given them warmth. The young ones do nothing but remember (meditate upon their mother. The tortoise's glance is, to the young ones, a downpour of nectar, the only source of sustenance and happiness. Similar is the relationship between the *Guru* and his disciples.

Humility

Humility is not towards all. Severity is necessary in dealing with the wicked.

Happiness

If others hate us, let us to take to *Nama japa* (chanting of God's name) and avoid them. Do not bark at people; do not be pugnacious. Bear with other's reproach. This is the way to happiness.

Help

If someone begs of anything and if that be in your hand or power and if you can grant the request, give it. Do not say, 'no', if you have nothing to give them, give a polite negative reply but do not mock or ridicule the applicant nor get angry with him.

Hospitality

No one comes to us without *Rinanubandha* (some previous bond of give and take). So when any dog, cat, pig, fly or person approaches you, do not drive it or him away with the words '*Hat-Hat*', '*Jit-Jit*'.

Inquiry

Inquire always: Who am I?

Introspection

We must see things for ourselves. What good is there in going about asking this man or that for his views and experiences?

Liberation

Service at the feet of *Guru* is essential to attain *moksha* (liberation).

Lust

A person who has not overcome lust cannot see (realize) God.

Name chanting

If you do this – chanting *'Raja-Ram'*, your mind will attain peace and you will be immensely benefitted.

Non-Possession

Everything belongs to us for use. Nothing is for us to possess.

Omnipresence

I am not confined within this body of three and a half cubic height; I am everywhere. See Me in every place.

Oneness

The dog which you saw before meals and to which you gave the piece of bread is one with Me, so also other creatures (cats, pigs, flies, cows, etc.) are one with Me. I am roaming in their forms. So abandon the sense of duality and serve Me as you did today (by feeding that dog).

Poverty

Poverty is the highest of riches and superior to Lord's position. God is brother of the poor. *Faqir* is the real emperor. *Faqir* does not perish, but empire is soon lost.

Quarrel

If anybody comes and abuses you or punishes you, do not quarrel with him. If you cannot endure it, speak a simple word or two, or else go away from that place. But do not battle with him and behave like this.

Questioning

Mere questioning is not enough. The question must not be made with any improper motive or attitude or to trap the Guru and catch him at mistakes in the answer, or out of idle curiosity. It must be with a view to achieving *moksha* or spiritual progress.

Reality

Brahma (God)is the only 'Reality' and the Universe is ephemeral and no one in this world, be he son, father or wife, is really our's.

Saints

Daily take *darshan* of *Siddhas*, i.e., perfect saints. Live a moral life. Then you will be pure evenin death.

Self-realization

The idea that "I am the body" is a great disillusion, and attachment to this ideas is the cause of bondage. Leave this idea and therefore the attachment, if you want to reach the goal of self-realization.

Service

Seva is not rendering service while still retaining the feeling that one is free to offer or refuse service. One must feel that he is not the master of the body, that the body is Guru's and exists merely to render service to Him.

Sin

Inflicting pain on others by body, mind and speech is (*paap*) sin, the reverse is merit, good.

Support

Come what may, stick to your Support i.e. *Guru*, and ever remain steady, always in union with Him.

Surrender

It is My special characteristics to free any person who surrenders completely to Me and who does worship Me faithfully and who remembers Me and meditates on Me constantly.

Truth

You should have truth always with you. Then I will be always with you, where-so-ever you are and at all times.

Unity

Rama and Rahim were one and the same; there was not the last difference between them; then why should their devotees full out and quarrel among themselves? You ignorant folk, children, join hands and bring both communities together, act sanely and thus you will gain your object of national unity.

Vicissitudes of Life

Gain and loss, birth and death, are in the hands of God. But how blindly people forget that God looks after life as long as it lasts!

Worldly Honour

Do not be deluded by worldly honour. The form of the deity should be firmly fixed in the mind. Let all the senses and mind be ever devoted to the worship of the Lord.

Ar treasure of Sri Shirdi Sai Baba's teachings was discovered in Sai Sharananand's Marathi book '*Sri Sai Baba* (1982). In its chapter 17, entitled *Sai Vani*, Swami Sharnananda had presented Sai Baba's original words of teaching. Baba used to speak in Marathi language. Hei had actually lived with Sri Sai Baba for some months, heard Him talking to devotees and giving them advice. Therefore, Baba's words of advice or teachings in their rustic flavor of Marathi of the masses and Hindustani language (mixture of Hindi, Urdu, Marathi, etc.) are not only very attractive but they penetrate our minds, hearts and souls instantly like arrows.

Some of the words of advice of Baba in original Marathi and Hindustani words – the actual words which Baba uttered to communicate to His devotees for the sake of their welfare – are reproduced below:

God

Allah malik hai, dursra koi nahin. Tyachi Karni alukik, amaulik, akal a'he.

("God is the Master, None else is the Master. His actions are supernatural, invaluable and full of wisdom.":

Gharibon ka Allah wali hai. Allah se bada koi nahin.

("God is the friend of the poor. There is none greater than *Allah* (God)."

Ishwar aahe hai, satya maanIshwar nahin hai, khote Samajh,Sab Allah hi.Allah hai,Ha sarva allah mian cha aahe.

"'God does exist' – consider it as truth,'There is no God' – consider it as false; Everything is God Everything belong to God."

God's-realizatio

Dev Kinnai lai Kanvalu aahe, aapnach tyahcyawar bharosa thewit nahin aani saburi pakrit nahin.

"It is not easy to realize God. Patience and strong determination are necessary to have the glimpse of God."

Brevity in Speech

Jyachyawar eshwari kripa hote to holte nahin;Pan jyachyawar eishwari avkripa hote to phaar bolte.

"Whoever is bestowed with the kindness of God does not speak; but absence of God's kindness makes a person speak unnecessarily."

On Himself

Ham kisike bande nahin hain. Allah ke banda hain.

"We are (I am) not servant of anyone; we are the servant of God."

Ham Gangapur mein bhi hain, Pandarpur mein bhi hain, sab thikana mein hain, sab jagah pe Ham hain aur Hamare paas sab jag hai.

"We are (I am) at Gangapur, We are at Pandarpur, we are at all places, and all placesa re with us."

Detachment

Dunya ikadchi tikre jhali tari apan maage pude hou nahin. Nishchal rahun Kautuk teware pahawe (Sakshiwat raha).

"All the world is full of pulls or problems, you keep on your path, remain unmoved by the curiosity; remain detached."

Poverty

Garibi awal baadshahi amiri se lakh sawai,Gharibon Ke Allah Hai,

"Poverty is first class kingship, it is better than richness, Allah is the brother of the poor."

Proper Conduct

Aakalaya gelebyacha aadar kar, trishitalla paani de, bhukelyas bhakr, udharvyas wastar, wa ghar nasleyas basawyas ausri dyavi mahanje Shribari trust holi.

"Welcome whosoever comes to your house, give water the thirsty, cloth to the naked, keep in you house the helpless; this will satisfy Sri Hari (God)."

How to Recognize God

Akkal se khuda pahchanna.

"Recognize God with intelligence."

Karma (Actions)

Achchi tarah se chalo, Allah achacha karta hai.Buri tarah se challenge to bura hota hai.

"Behave properly; *Alla*h will do good (to you). Behave improperly, then only bad will happen (to you)."

Jaise jo karil, taise to bharil.

"As you sow, so shall you reap."

Neki ka phal bhari hai.Badi ka phal kam hai." The fruit of *neki* (good actions) is heavy, the fruit of bad (bad actions) is light.*Jashi jyachi neeyat tashi tyachi barkat.*

"As are one's motives, so are the results of his actions."

Jyacha irada changla tyache sagle chagle. Aapule karam apulya sange,dujiyache to dujiya sange.

"Your actions go it with you, Other's actions go with them."

Good conduct

Konchi barobari karu nahin; konachi ninda,Konchiya bolnyane apalyakaru nahin.

"Do not complete with anyone else;do not speak ill of anyone else."

Contentment

Yo jaisa rakhega waisa rehna.

Live as He(God) keeps you."

Gratitude to God

Allah peksha kauni meetha nahin. To kaunya tene jeevdaan deyil? Kaunya tene sambhalil, he tyache tayalach thauk?

"None is greater than God. Who gave you this life, who looked after you, who keeps you well?"

Tyachya Marjeet apan raji rahwe; talmal karu nahin. Tyachyashiwae jharache paan halat nahin.

"We should be contented with whatever He wishes of us, we should not grudge; without God's wish not even a leaf of tree can flutter."

Aaple kartwya apan karawwe, pan kartepanacha aabhamaan aaplykare na gheta kartatwa parmeshwarale dhyawe, aani phal hi tyasach arpan karawe, mahanje aapn alpit rahun karam aapleyala haadhak honal nahin.

"Everyone should do his duty without any ego, surrendering the fruit to God; thus it results in his detachment from the fruit."

Tolerance

Angala bhoke parat nahit.

"Bear whatever anybody says, for it doesn't hurt the body."

Prayer

Kasht karin aasawe, tikene rahu nahin,

Devache nauw dhyane, pothi puran vachawe,

Aahar vihar tyage nahit, pan niyamit aasawe.

"If you are in a problem, do not sit idle lost in it; pray to God, read old scriptures, do not fast but regulate your food habits."

God's Wish

Eshwar karel tech hoil, tyacha raasta toch dakhwil aani vina vilambh manachi muraad pur hoil.

"Whatever God wishes, that will happen. He will open the door and let you enter it; He will fulfil your wishes without any delay."

Evil

> *Bure se Khuda dare aur Khuda se bura dare.*
> "God is afraid of evil doer, and evil doer is afraid of God."

God's Omnipotence

> *Parameshwar aahe wa tyachya peksha kauni motha nahin.*
> *To sarv chara-chara madhye bharun urla aahe.Utpan nahin toch karito, rakhi tohitoch,Barhwit tohi toch, aani mari toh toch,To thewil tase rahawe*
> "None is greater than God who is omnipresent and omnipotent, who has given you birth, Who has nurtured you, who alone kills you; as He keeps you, you remain."

Love

> *Sarv bhut matranshi premaane wagawe.Waadawaadi karu nahin, koni kahi bolle tari ekun dhyawe.*
> "Treat all with love; do not argue, do not unnecessarily talk with others, concentrate on Him."

Right thinking

> *ratyekane nekane waagaaweSadsadhichar shakti jagrit thewavi.*
> "Guide everyone on the right path; develop right thinking."

Sri Shirdi Sai Baba's Messages

Although Shirdi Sai Baba achieved *Maha Nirvana* in 1918, His valuable messages have been received by His real devotees who may be many I know about three most fortunate ones among such recipients of His grace:

- Zoroastrian Yogi M.K.Spencer of Karachi
  He received 77 messages from the Spirit of Shirdi Sai Baba. during 3.11.52-18.2.53 which he had recorded in his major work of spiritual memoirs entitled *"How I Found God"*(1957) which has been edified by me and published by New Age Books, New Delhi in 2013 under ISBN 978-81-82-7822-352-0.

The themes of those 77 rare Sai messages are as under;

1. In the stily silence of night; The panorama of Nature
2. From darkness into Light
3. Evil has no rigid place in God's kingdom
4. Renunciations the essence of spirituality
5. Religion is the soul's nourishment
6. God knows no language except of the heart, soul and spirit
7. Peace, harmony and form the rhyme of life
8. Who is superman? One who pus on armour of righteousness
9. Self effacement is the flower of perfection
10. What is the goal of life? God
11. Gain in mastery of the soul and mind
12. Righteousness – the most potent factor in life
13. Break the chain of Maya with the hammer of self-consciousness
14. The greater the trial, the greater the reward
15. Seek the hidden light
16. The ladder of evolution – inequalities in life
17. Death and the sinner
18. Religion and the origin of evil
19. Control of Mind
20. Trample the sin but do not despise the sinner
21. The Chariot and the charioteer
22. Prayers and their significance
23. As you sow shall you reap
24. God not an enigma
25. How an invisible can become visible
26. Seek God through the gateways of renunciation and devotion
27. God realization – the goal of life not earthly happiness
28. The uncertainty of life, there is one certainty – God
29. Grow in spirit
30. Don't make life a tomb of woe and wantonness
31. Be a brave worrier in the battle of life
32. Saints and sages
33. God's love and light
34. Make life a saga, an epic of heroism M, M
35. Silence – the language ofternity

70. Spirit us the richness of soul, it alone survives
71. All things change in the universe except God
72. No real peace unless man ventures to tread the rugged path and reaches the path of God-realization
73. Man's intellect however powerful is of no avail in perceiving the over soul
74. Spiritual knowledge not be criteria of man's accessibility to God but his own sincerity and Spirituality
75. The occult science
76. What is vital is spirit
77. The essence of everything is God 1983)

- Sri Umamaheswar Rao of Guntur
  He was a retired Police officer Sri Umamaheswar Rao. He first visited Shirdi in 1980, and then many Sai miracles happened in his life. Messages from the Supreme Spirit Sri Shirdi Sai Baba started coming to him from that year. His life was saved By Sai Baba when he suffered heart attack in November 1983,then again heart attack in January 1987; in February 1992 he was bitten by a cobra at Tirupati, in 1991 he was caught in mysterious fire while doing meditation and later on he died while *Sai Nam japa* and Dutta worship,as advised by Sai Baba in an urgent message from the Spirit of Sai Baba while visiting Sri Sai Samadhi Mandir,at Shirdi,and later on in innumerable dreams and daily meditation sessions from 1980 till he merged in Sai Baba at 3 P.M. on 4th February,!9990 in the presence of bout 400 devotees.

He had received more than 100 messages and discourses on Sai Baba's unique spiritual philosophy, As s instructed by the Supreme Spirit of Sai Baba, he faithfully compiled hem in his three very important books- *'Bhava Lahari'* (*'Spiritual Philosophy of Sri Shirdi Sai Baba', Thus This Sri Shirdi Sai Baba' and 'Communications from the Spirit of Sri Shirdi Sai Baba.'* All these three invaluable spiritual books were later on edited by me in 1998 as desired, duly permitted and their copyrights transferred to me by him vide his letter of 31st October,1997. I gave them to Diamond Pocket Books, they have reached countess Sai devotees in over 80 countries since1998.

Now in 2015 all the three of them have been compiled and re-edited by me in one comprehensive book entitled *'Unique Spiritual Philosophy of Sri Shirdi Sai Baba'* which is being published by Notion Press,Chennai (publish@ notionpress.

A few sample Sai messages received by (Late) B.Umamaheswar Rao are given below:

➢ "I am the *'Parasakti'* and I am the *'Adi Sakti'* who created Brahma, Vishnu and *Maheswrara*. I am the one,who is the cause of creation and dissolution. I am the mother of the universe. Those who realize Me as *Brahman* (God)will nor receive my blssings,but shal alsoi be their constnt companion. Shall asolve aallthos who chant my name from bondage as well as free temfrom death…"

➢ "I am the seed of all beings,Whatever exists in thisworld –living or nonliving-,none of them can be, if *were* not."

➢ "Those who remember my lotus feet and worship Me,I shall free them from *agyan*";;

➢ "I am only witness like the sun. I am neither attached nor reattached to anyone.reaps what he sows according to his thoughts, words and deeds. This is the divine law that applies to all"

➢ Whatever work you do, do it with full devotion.ake your life fruitful. Do not lose balance on getting happiness or unhappiness. They both are always together.'.

➢ "Learn to sympathize with bad people and also those who follow the path of *adhama* (9unrighteousness),".

➢ "Do not blow your own trumpet. Boasting betrays your emptiness. Truth has no trumpet"

➢ *"Nishkama Karma"* is essential for spiritual practice *(Sadhana).* Conquer your mind with your mind itself. To those who surrender to Me, concentrate their mind on Me, attain Divine grace *(Jnana Yoga Abhista Siddhi)*, I undoubtedly reveal Myself completely. Then they would grasp what I am.

➢ There is no way for those who doubt Me. If one wants to reach the goal and attain salvation, one should hold on to Me tightly. Drop the desires for worldly pleasures and dry to seek joyous self. Then only you will achieve *BRAHMA SUKHANUBHUTHI.* Don't think that salvation is elsewhere and comes from somewhere else, Salvation is right here and within. Don't be elevated by pleasures and depressed by hardships, but keep your mind and firm intellect *(Sthira Buddhi)* in Me.

➤ "Do your allotted duties *(Vihitha Karma)* always without aspiring for the results. Keep your mind free from likes and dislikes *(Raga-Dvesha)*. Purity of mind is attained through *Karmas* done without seeking its results. Grief and hardships are not caused by *Karma* but by attachment of bonds of passion. Get rid of selfishness. Don't be fond of body which leads to ego. Do not let selfish thoughts and passions come near you. If you are free of them, you can do any *Karma* even while you are in '*Sansara*'. This is '*Vairagya*' (detachment*)*

On the internet

On the internet, the following links to the messages of Sri Shirdi SaI Baba are available, they may be gathered by the interested readers:

- <u>Message from the teachings of Shri Shirdi Saibaba for today</u> <u>https://www.facebook.com/.../Message...Shirdi-Saibaba.../2019543</u> <u>02799</u>
- Message from the teachings of Shri Shirdi Saibaba for today. 18704 likes ·7609 talking about this. Blog dedicated to Shri Shirdi Saibaba...
- Experience the Magic by sharing Shirdi Sai Baba's Daily Messages and Teachings from Shree Sai Satcharitra. mysai.org.Most Relevant
- Sh Shirdi Sai Baba Answers n solves problems <u>www.yoursaibaba.com/</u>
- <u>Message from the teachings of Shri Shirdi Saibaba for todayhttps://</u> <u>www.facebook.com/.../Message...Shirdi-Saibaba.../201954302799</u>
- Experience the Magic by sharing Shirdi Sai Baba's Daily Messages and Teachings from Shree Sai Satcharitra. mysai.org. Like Comment Share. Most Relevant.
- Shirdi Sai Baba, solves your problem. its a Miracle, Your Sai Baba will Answer ... The Miracle here is that Shirdi Sai Baba will answer your questions. .... This website is completely dedicated to Shirdi Saibaba & is meant to spread his message.
- <u>Selection of 100 Shirdi Sai Baba Sayings</u>
- www.saibaba.ws/quotes/shirdi100sayings.htm

- Message from the teachings of Shri Shirdi Saibaba for today
  https://www.facebook.com/.../Message...Shirdi-SaiBaba..

Message from the teachings of Shri **Shirdi Saibaba** for today.. Blog dedicated to Shri **Shirdi Saibaba**...

Sai Baba's Blessings - Facebook

https://www.facebook.com/srisaibaba

Experience the Magic by sharing **Shirdi Sai Baba's** Daily **Messages** and Teachings from Shri Sai Satcharitra. mysai.org. Like Comment Share. Most Relevant.

Photos - Ganesha Blessings - About - Friendship Stamps

Shirdi Sai Baba Answers questions n solves problems ...

www.yoursaibaba.com/

Shirdi Sai Baba, solves your problem. its a Miracle, Your **Sai Baba** will Answer ... The Miracle here is that **Shirdi Sai Baba** will answer your questions. .... This website is completely dedicated to **Shirdi Saibaba** & is meant to spread his **message**.

Selection of 100 Shirdi Sai Baba Sayings

www.**saibaba**.ws/quotes/**shirdi**100sayings.htm

A Collection from Sri **Sai** Satcharita Why fear when I am here? I am formless and everywhere. I am in everything and beyond. I fill all space. All that you see ...

Saibaba shirdi Vision blessings teachings of shirdi saibaba

www.star**sai**.com/about-star**sai**/

Shirdi saibaba visions teachings and blessings of **shirdi sai baba**. ... Spreading the**message** of humanity and the divine path of **Shirdi saibaba** : As a graduate in ...

Shirdi saibaba chant sai sai sai for blessings

www.**shirdisai**chant.com/

shirdi saibaba blessings by chanting sai sai sai regularly. ... the importance of saying "sai sai sai", it means **shirdi saibaba** wants me to spread this **message**.

MySai.Org - My Home on the Web

https://www.my**sai**.org/

Org contains many features like teachings from *Satcharitra*, Live Darshan from **Shirdi, Sai Baba** Prashanavali, Daily **Messages** from Sri Satcharitra and much ...

Sri Sai Baba, Quote of the day, SaiMail

www.**saibaba**.com/

Sri **Saibaba**, Holy **Shirdi**, **Saibaba** Mandirs, Sai Literature, The Blessed Ones, Sai Knowledge Base, Quote of the day, Sai Kids, Saipatham, Sai Aratis, SaiMail, ...

Shirdi Sai Baba SMS Shayari collection 2014 - Avnavu

avnavu.com 'Hindi

Aug 31, 2014 - **Shirdi Sai Baba** SMS Shayari collection 2014. sai babaji sms ... Sai**message** to all SMS Shayari **Shirdi Sai Baba** Hindi Shayari Sai Wish to all ...

The teachings and messages of Sri Sai Baba are so direct, transparent and lucid that they are immediately assimilated by every person irrespective of his religion, caste, class, sex, nationality and the like. None of these teachings and messages smacks of fundamentalism or parochialism; none of them portrays the zeal of a religious propagandist and his intense wish to proselytize or convert people by terrorizing them with the fear of hell or nemesis. All these teachings are essentially the finest and uniquely distilled rich contents of the spirituality and morality which all the religions, codes of good conduct and all the finest examples of culture have developed so far. These teachings give the essential quality of soothing or calming the agonies of the human heart and cementing all differences. They are truly conjunctive integrating and noble.

At the time of descent of Sri Shirdi Sai Baba on the world scene, India was groaning under the atrocities and exploitation of the British; it was seething with discontent and remorse as a result of the failure of the First Battle of India's Independence led by such great patriots as Rani Laxmi Bai of Jhansi (in whose army Sri Shirdi Sai Baba also served for a few months in 1857), Nana Phadnavees, Bahadur Shah Zafar, etc. On top of it, the mutual jealousies and disunity were eating up the very vitals of Indian Society due to the poisonous cankers of casteism, Hindu-Muslim hatred, diehard ritualism and exploitation by the Brahmins. There was a serious crisis which could not be averted by either the propagation of a new religion or any movement for the mass conversion of the Hindus as the Muslim fanatics were trying or that of the Muslims of Hinduism as Swami Dayanand, a contemporary of Sri Shirdi Sai Baba, was advocating enthusiastically. These teachings of Sri Shirdi Sai Baba served as a natural, simple, rustic and magical panacea to all the moral and cultural maladies of the ailing, decaying and tormented Indian society.

Chapter – 4

Sri Shirdi Sai Baba's Contemporary Devotees

"I will not allow My devotes to come to harm. I have to take thought for My devotees. And if a devotee is about to fall, I stretch My hands, and thus with four outstretched hands at a time support him. I will let him fall."

- Sri Shirdi Sai Baba

Countless people came to Shirdi to seek the *darshan* and blessings of Sai Baba during His stay there from 1858 to 1918. It is virtually impossible to discover and recall the names of all those blessed souls. However, two most authoritative publications *'Shri Sai Sat Charita'* and *'Devotees Experiences of Sri Sai Baba'* (in which about 80 contemporary Sai of devotees, testimonies have been recorded) mention the names of hundreds of devotees of Sri Shirdi Sai Baba with whom miracle/s or notable experience/s had happened due to the blessings of Baba. Surely, their experience had happened due to the blessings of Baba. Surely, there might be many other people of Shirdi and visitors from outside who were also recipients of Baba's grace, but they have gone unknown and their experiences could not be recorded by early biographers and authors of books on Baba.

Who became Sri Shirdi Sai Baba's Devotees?

One may say that outwardly innumerable people of various places, different religions and castes and varying social and cultural strata became attracted towards Shirdi Sai Baba and so they came to Him. But the reality, as revealed by Baba Himself, was different. Accordingly to Him, only the following were coming to Him to become His devotees.

(i)   Those souls with whom He had close *rinanubandha* (connections) from their several previous births.

(ii) Those souls whom He wanted to pull near Him in order to guide, help, transform or liberate.

(iii) Those souls whom He Himself wanted to come near; none could ever, just on his own, intrude.

The following quotation of Baba clearly substantiate these points:

"I draw My man to Me, wherever and however far he might be like a sparrow with a string tied to its legs.I will willy-nilly drag anyone who is My man, even if he is in the seventh nether world."

Sri Sai Sat Charita mentions:

'Onee peculiarity of Shirdi pilgrims was that none could leave Shirdi without Baba's permission and if they did, invited untold sufferings; but if one was asked to leave Shirdi, he could stay there no longer. Baba gave certain suggestions or hints when *bhaktas* (devotees) went to bid Him goodbye and to take His leave.

Like a very powerful magnet, Baba pulled towards Him a number of highly blessed souls with whom He had been associated in many previous lives. To the following devotees Baba had clearly revealed that they had been with Him for a number of past births:

*Mlahaspati:*Many births

*Shama:*72 births

*Nana Saheb Chandorkar:*4 births

*Raghuvir Parandhare:*7 centuries

*Professor G.G. Narke:*30 births

*Hemadpant:*30 births

*Upasani Mahara:*Thousands of years.

Sai Baba told Upasani Maharaj these words of revelation: "There is *rinanubandha* between us. Our families have been closelyconnected for thousand of years. So we are one."

*Mrs. Chandra Bai Borker:*7 births. Baba said: "She is asister of mine for 7 births."

Boy *Pishya*: "Pishya was a Rohilla in his previous birth,a very good man who prayed aloud and once came as a guest to my (Sai Baba's) grandfather.The latte rhad a sister who used to live separately. I (Sai Baba) was a young boy then and I had playfully suggested that the Rohilla should marry her. Later he did so. The Rohilla lived these with his wife for a long time and ultimately went away with her, nobody knowswhere. He died and I (Sai Baba) put him in the womb of the present mother."

Baba revealed this to Khaparde:

He (Sai Baba) told the story of a former birth in which He, Bapu Sahib Jog, Dada Kelkar, Madhavarao Deshpande (Shama), and Dixit were associated and lived in a blind alley. There was His *Murshid* (Guru) there. "He has now brought us together again." Referring to another birth, Baba told, "You were with Me for two or three years, and went into royal service, though there was enough at home to live in comfort."

Baba revealed about Mrs. Lakshmi G. Khaparde's past lives as under:

"In one of her previous births she was a very fat cow yielding much milk and belonged to a merchant. Thereafter I lost sight of her (for some time) and in the birth which followed she was born to a gardener, then to a Kshatriya and thereafter became the wife of a merchant. Later, she was born in a Brahmin family and now he has been sighted after a long time. Let Me partake the food (served by her now) happily with love and give her satisfaction.

This clearly shows that Baba had pulled many of His dear ones of previous births to Him as devotees at Shirdi. The second point that Baba pulled His men towards Him mysteriously is proved by the case studies of Baba's eminently known close devotees like Mlahaspati, Bade Baba (alias Bade *Mian alias* Fakir Pir Mohammed Yasin Mian), Chand Bhai Patil, Abdul, Das Ganu, Nana Saheb Chandorkar, Kaka Dixit, Dabholkar 'Hemadpant', Dhumal, Shama, Radha Krishna Ayi, Sai Sharananada, etc.

Mlahaspati: He was a hereditary goldsmith and the priest of Khandoba Temple of Shirdi. He welcomed Baba and gave the name 'Sai' to Him in 1858 and served and worshipped Him with matchless devotion till Baba's *Maha*

Nirvana in 1918. "In fact, not only was he first, in point of time, amongst the worshippers, but he was also the foremost in excellence."

Bade Baba: This Muslim *faqir* who was older than Baba in age,was the first devotee of Sai Baba. Baba and instructed and helped him at a mosque in Aurangabad for some years during 1854-58, i.e., before Baba came to Shirdi for the second time and settled there permanently. In later years, this *faqir* was pulled by Sai Baba to His *Dwarka Mai Masjid* in 1909 and he lived with Baba till His *Maha Nirvana* in 1918. Baba used to give him the maximum amount of daily gift (Rs.30/- to 55/-) out of His daily collection of donations from visitors to Dwaraka Mai.Chand Bhai Patil: He was the rich Nawab of Dhoopkheda village. He was the first devotee of Baba who had witnessed the miracles done by Baba. Baba drew him towards Himself in a mysterious way. In 1858, Baba was seated under a *mango* tree in a forest near the twin villages Sindhon-Bindhon. Chand Bhai, who was searching for his lost mare 'Yad' for the past two months, passed that way. Baba attracted him by showing three miracles in no time – showing the whereabouts of the lost mare which was found to be grazing near a stream nearby, materializing a live ember and then materializing water to wet a cloth for clay-pipe. Baba went with him to Shirdi along with the marriage party of his nephew.

Abdul: in 1889, Baba appeared in the dream of a Muslim *faqir*, Aminuddin of Nanded, and materialized two mangoes and asked him to give the two mangoes to Abdul, and send Him immediately to serve Him at Shirdi. Abdul served Baba till His *Maha Samadhi*, doing all kinds of services for Sai Baba, like filling water in pitchers, filling oil in lamps, cleaning the *Dwarka Mai Masjid* and, street in the front of the mosque, washing Baba's clothes, etc., Baba transformed him and told him:

"I have enabled you to cross the river."

"I have turned your clay into gold."

By his dedicated service towards Baba and Baba's constant guidance and training, Abdul emerged as an eminent devotee and a saint.

Das Ganu: (6.1.1868-25.11.1962): Ganpatrao Dattatreya Sahasrabuddhe, a Brahmin of Akolner village, became a sepoy (policeman) in 1891 and later became a Havaldar. He took great interest in *tamashas* (village plays) of erotic and sometimes obscene nature and even took part in them. He composed poems, often impromptu. Baba advised himto resign thevpolice job, but he geglected His advice. Then Baba created a situation which forced him to resign in 1903 and come to the shelter at Baba's feet. He was implicated in a false misappropriation case, but by Baba's divine intervention he was saved. He spent the rest of his life in performing *kirtans* and composing devotional poems and prayers in praise of Sri Shirdi Sai Baba. It was for him that Baba did the well known miracle of materializing the holy water of Ganga from His toes which He sprinkled on his head. However, he did not drink that holy water as he thought that being a Brahmin he would be polluted by drinking the washing of Baba's feet as *tirath* (holy water). Despite his faults and foibles, Das Ganu was one of the notable followers of Baba whose base metal of a petty-minded lewd followers of Baba whose base metal of a petty-minded lewd constable was turned into gold of a saint, who in turn moulded the spiritual destinies of tens of thousands of Sai devotees by his *kirtans*. In his thrilling testimony, he has vividly recalled the miracles, behaviour patterns and teachings of Baba.

Nana Saheb Chandorkar: Narayan Govind Chandorkar, a pious high-caste Hindu, was the *chitins* of the district collector of Ahmednagar. Baba who knew him from his last four births in which he had been Baba's disciple, sent for him twice but he considered it below his dignity to go to meet a Muslim *fakir* living in an old and dilapidated mosque of a small village like Shirdi. Ultimately, the Collector's order to him to go to Shirdi to make villagers agree to get themselves inoculated and his police subordinate Das Ganu's entreaties to visit Sai Baba of Shirdi to seek His blessings for his barren daughter Maina Tai, impelled Nana Saheb to come to Baba's shelter in 1903. In 1904, Baba did the famous miracle of materializing a horse carriage with its driver and servant to carry Baba's messenger Ramgir Bua (with whom Baba had sent His *udi* (holy ash) and *aarti*(worship prayer) to ensure safe delivery of Maina Tai) to the Deputy Collector of Jamner, Nana Saheb Chandorkar. Nana Saheb spent the rest of his life in dedicated devotion and service to Baba. He served Baba's institution, Sri Sai Baba Samsthan, Shirdi, after the *Maha Nirvana* of Baba, for many years till his death. Baba loved him very much and used to have spiritual discussions with him. He watched the promotion of his spiritual and temporal welfare. Many of the great teachings of Baba came to be known to the world only through Nana Saheb. He was the only devotee who was always privileged to sit very close to Sai Baba in the *Dwarka Mai Masjid*. Narasimhaswamiji, has however commented that "His (Nana Saheb's) faith in Baba was undoubtedly very great, but still his constitution, or the degree of progress made by him, prevented him from getting lost into Baba."

Kaka Dixit (1864-5.7.1926): Hari Sitaram Dixit, a high caste Nagari Brahim of Khandwa, did B.A., LLB, and became a leading solicitor of Bombay. He was the Secretary of the Indian National Congress of 1904 at Bombay. In 1906, on his visit to England he had an accident in London whch caused him an injury in the leg with constantly pained. Nana Chandorkar advised him in 1909 to go to Shirdi and seek Sai Baba's blessings. The same year he went to Ahmednagar with some work and was a guest in the house of Sardar Kaka Saheb Mirikar who was the devotee of Sai Baba. Baba had his own my mysterious way of bringing Kaka Saheb to Him. Baba's close devotee, Shama, had gone to Ahmednagar to see his ailing mother-in-law. He went to Mirikar's house to meet him. Mirikar gave him a photo of Baba which was reframed for Megha. He asked Shama to take Kaka Saheb to Shirdi to see Sai Baba. Thus he reached the Divine feet of Sai Baba comfortably. Kaka Dixit rendered great service to Baba and His sansthan by his skill and wisdom. "Dixit offered his *tan* (body), *man* (mind), *dhan* (wealth) at his Guru's (Baba) feet with perfect confidence. He gave up practice as well as society, politics, socializing, etc., which were dear to him in former days, and stuck to Shirdi to render service to Baba and the *bhaktas*, both before and after 1918 upto the very end of his life. He died peacefully, remembering Baba's name on the auspicious *Ekadashi* day on 5 July, 1926, travelling in Bombay train in the company of Anna Saheb Dabolkar. Baba had appeared in his dream on the previous night.

Hemadpant: Anna Saheb Dabolkar, whom Baba gave the honorable nickname of "Hemadpant" was chosen by Baba to be the blessed biographer of Baba, the author of *Shri Sai Sat Charita*. He was a chosen a Brahmin from a poor family. He was a self-made man. Having studied only up to class five and after passing the public service examination, he joined service as a humble village *talati* and rose to the position of *Mamlatdar* and first class Magistrate by dint of his ability. In 1910, he was drawn to Sai Baba's feet in Shirdi. He was fortunate to receive Baba's permission in 1916 and encouragement to write *Shri Sai Sat Charita* in Marathi which ran into more than a thousand pages. It was later translated into Hindi, English and other languages. After his retirement in 1916, he rendered a great service to Baba and His Sansthan. Baba enabled him to achieve great spiritual advancement by showering His grace on him.

Dhumal: S.B. Dhumal was leading lawyer of Nasik. He became a devotee of Gajanan Maharaj in 1903 and was drawn to Sri Sai Baba of Shirdi in

1907. Baba's immense blessings were experienced by him to his personal and professional life and spiritual advancement. Baba once told him, "At every step I am taking care of you. If I did not, what would become of you, God alone knows. On another occasion, Baba told him *"Bhau,* the whole of last night, I had no sleep…I was thinking and thinking of you all the night." He was instrumental in winning the legal cases of Baba's devotees like Raghu. He was of a great service to Baba and His Sansthan.

Shama: Madhavrao Deshpande *alias* 'Shama' (the name of Baba gave him) was, according to Baba's revelation to him living in the same lane with the Baba in many former birth. He was a school teacher in the primary school in Shirdi, a window of which always looked on to the adjoining Dwarka Mai Masjid of Sai Baba. In the beginning, he used to think that Baba was a mad *faqir* and he used to hear voices in English, Hindi, Marathi, Urdu, and many other languages coming from the Masjid at night. Later on he got attracted towards Baba to such an extent that he left service and was attached to Him whole time. He was witness to all His miracles, teachings and actions and He represented Baba in a number of functions and feasts hosted by Baba's devotees. Baba loved him most and was very free with him. His memoirs of Baba throw a great deal of valuable light on His divine life.

Radha Krishna Ayi: She was a Brahmin widow who was deeply devoted to Baba. After her husband's death she migrated from Ahmednagar to her maternal grandfather. Advocate Baba Saheb Ganesh's house in Shirdi to spend the rest of her life in devoted service to Sai Baba. She served Baba by cleaning the *Masjid* and *chawdi* as well as scavenging the street and serving and providing food to every visitor or devotee Baba sent to her house. Her house was considered to be *Shala* (school) for training Baba's devotees for she was a strict disciplinarian, harsh in speech, yet very spiritual and hard working as well as a hard taskmaster. "She had wonderful powers of thought reading and clairvoyance. When some unusual order came from Baba that such and such a dish was wanted, she would keep it ready and supply it once…She was deeply devoted to Sai Baba, and rendered a great service to His Sansthan. She had a very sharp tongue and many found her incompanionable. But Sai Baba put his devotees there to perhaps develop their power of endurance.

Devotee Raghuvir B. Purandhare in his memoirs has recalled about her:

"I spent every minute of my time at Shirdi in service to Sai Baba, in accordance with the directions of Ayi. She made me work hard all day long for Baba mostly at her residence, often at *Masjid* and elsewhere. Radha Krishna Ayi was a personality of a strange sort. She would sing charmingly and with deep emotion. Suddenly, she would break into laughter or melt into tears and either continue slowly with choked voice or stop the song altogether by her sobs."

Another devotee, Chinna Krishna Raja Saheb Bahadur, has given this profile of Radha Krishna Ayi:

"Ayi was a noble and affectionate person – an "Ayi" or mother indeed… She used to get a *roti* (bread) from Baba as *prasad* daily. She lived only for Baba and her delight was to carry out everything that He wanted or was needed for His Sansthan, i.e., institution and devotees. I find that Baba's instructions and help to me came through Ayi, in a peculiar way. Ayi was so open-hearted and kind that from the first day I could confide all my views and plans to her, and she revealed her ideas and plans to me. As for religious progresses, she said that we should so act that no other person should guess what we are doing and and how we are getting on.

…As for religious exercise, Ayi was an excellent singer with a divinely charming voice and a good knowledge of music. She could play on sitar…She said that many used the name of Vittal Ram, etc., but that so far as she was concerned, "Sai" was her God and that name was sufficient for her, while I might go on with the Vittal, etc., if I chose."

Ayi died serving Baba wholeheartedly in 1916 and was cremated on the bank of Godavari river about 8 kms from Shirdi.

Sai Sharnananda: Sri Wamanbhai Prangovind Patel, popularly known Sai Sharnananda, was born in 1889 in a small village in Bardoli Taluka of Gujarat State. As a boy of 7-8 years on a visit to Somnath Temple he saw a *fakir* whom he saw several times afterwards and on his first visit to Shirdi on 11 December, 1911 he was surprised to see the same *faqir* in Sai Baba. He passed LLB. examination in 1912, joined a solicitor's firm, became principal of Model High School, Ahmedabad, and in 1921 became a managing clerk in a solicitor's firm in Bombay. In 1923, he took *sanyas* and served Sai *Sansthan*(Trust) at Shirdi. He was privileged to inaugurate Baba's marble statue in *Samadhi Mandir* at Shirdi in 1952 which had been sculptured by the famous sculptor, Bhalaji Vasant Talim of Bombay. His book *Sai Sai The Superman* is a remarkable book on Bbaa. Baba had once revealed that Sharnananda and Balakram Mankad in a previous life resided opposite each other in caves doing penance. In 1913, Baba detained him at Shirdi and asked him to do *Gayatri Purascharan* (continuous recitation of **Gayatri Mantra**) to wipe off the sins of his past *karmas*. Baba used to send him to beg food on His behalf and collect donations from visitors and devotees in Shirdi on a number of occasions.

Upasant Maharaj (15.5.1870-24.12.1941): A doyen among Baba's closest devotees was Kashinath Upasani upon whom Baba wanted to bestow all His divine powers and make him a great saint like Him. Baba had revealed to him that he and Baba had closely associated in innumerable births for thousands of years. He was drawn to Baba on 27th June, 1911. He underwent spiritual training under Sai Baba's strict vigilance. This was a period of fiery ordeal accompanied by fasting, blindness for sometime, physical mortification, insult and other forms of austerities. "Sri Sai helped His *Shishya*(disciple)Kashinath in many ways, to see that he (Kashinath) lost attachment with his body. He showed him to previous *janmas* (birth) and the various forms he had inhabited. So he was none of those bodies, and neither the *papa purusha* nor his *punya purusha*, but distinct from them all. Baba told this about him to one Prabhu from Bombay who was jealous of Baba's declaration that He had given everything to the stranger Upasani:

Prabhu: "What, Baba, we have been attending upon You for years, and You seem to be conferring a copper plate grant, and are we all, therefore, to be neglected? Is it true that You are giving all our powers?"

Baba: "Yes, speak only the truth sitting as I do in this *Masjid*. What I have spoken, I have spoken, have given everything to this person.Whether he be good or bad, he is My own. Iam fully responsible for him and as for *sanad* or grant, why a copper grant? I have given him a gold plate grant.

Turning to Kashinath, Baba said, "Think,which is better, copper or gold? Kashinath: "I do not know, Baba."

Baba: "See, copper gets corroded and tarnished. Gold does not. Gold remains pure always. You are pure. You are pure *Bhagavan* (God)."

However, Upasani Maharaj could not bear the ordeal of Baba's training for long, and left Shirdi in the night of 25 July, 1914. He reached Scinde, Nagpur, Kharagpur and delivered discourses. The he returned to Sakori, a village near Shirdi, and established his famous institution "Kanya Kumari Sansthan, Sakori" for the spiritual regeneration of womenhood.

Mataji Krishna Priya: A resident of Nagpur, she worshipped Shirdi Sai Baba as Krishna and frequently visited Shirdi to seek Baba's blessings. Once she visited Shimla. She came to know that Baba had achieved *Maha Nirvana* immediately on 15 October, 1918 at 2.30 p.m. The next day, Shirdi Sai Baba appeared in His resurrected form at her cottage and accepted her hospitality of tea and food, blessed her and left the cottage. Her thrilling story has been revealed by Sri Sathya Sai Baba recently in his discourse on 27 September, 1992.

The above brief profiles of twelve most prominent devotees of Sri Shirdi Sai Baba who were closest to Him have been presented above. There were, however, many other well known devotees such as – Chinna Krishna Raja Saheb, Professor G.G. Narke, *Sanyasi* Narayan Asram, Abdulla Jan, M.V. Pradhan, Rai Bahadur Hari Vinayak Sathe, Damodar Salu Ram Rasane, Ram Chandra Sita Ram Deo, Balwant Kohojkar, Shama Rao Jaykar Painter, Imam Bhai, Chote Khan, Bayaja Bai, Laxmi Bai, Mrs. Tarkhad, Ram Gir Bua, Tatya, Sagun Meru Naik, K.J. Bhishma, Rajamma alias Shivamma Thayee, etc. These people and innumerable others like them were pulled by Shirdi Sai Baba towards Him on a variety of pretexts and means as their souls had to be given the final liberation push by Him.

Chapter – 5

Sri Shirdi Sai Baba's Contemporary Saints

"Saints exist to give devotees temporal and spiritual benefits. I have come to give such good things to the devotees."

-Sri Shirdi Sai Baba

When Sri Shirdi Sai Baba incarnated as *Avatar*, whole galaxy of saints also had to take birth and function as saints, as spiritualcollaborators or adjuncts of Sri Sai Baba in the divine drama during the later half of the 19th century and the beginning of the 20th century.Naturally our curiosity is awakened at this point. Sri Shirdi Sai Baba wasone of the Five Perfect Masters: who then were the other Four Perfect Masters?Aiyer has not given answer to it directly, but in his book *Perfect Masters* he gaveprofiles of Upasani Baba, Tajuddin Baba, Baba Jan, Narsing Maharaj and Meher Baba besides Sri Shirdi Sai Baba. That means, he mentioned five instead of four Perfect Masters.Bhardawaj cited a very interesting revelation in this connection:

"One day at 6:00 a.m., when he (Mankewala) was lying awake in bed Baba (SriShirdi Sai Baba) appeared before him and said, "I am not a fakir, I am the *avatar* of Lord Dattatreya. The same Lord is carrying on his divine mission assuming thedifferent forms of Tajuddin Baba of Nagpur, Dhunivale Dada of Khandwa, SriVesnudevananda Saraswathi of Narmada, Sri Swami Samartha of Akkalkot andmyself."

Sri Shirdi Sai Baba As Avatar Of Lord Shiva

Sri Sathya Sai, who claimd to be the incarnation of Sri Shirdi Sai Baba,revealed that Lord Shiva had incarnated as Sri Sai Baba of Shirdi.15 In this connection,

The following extract from B.V. Narasimhaswami ji, the well-known protagonistof Baba's name, is worth serious consideration: "The Supreme Being is thought of as having five aspects or functions withnames appropriate to each:

Creation: Brahma in conjunction with Saraswati.
Maintenance: Vishnu or Narayana in conjunction with Lakshmi.
Destruction: Rudra in conjunction with Kali.
Protection or: Iswara (Shiva) inRuling conjuction with Maheswari.
Redemption: Sadashiv in conjuction with Kripa.

There are *avatars* combining often several of these elements. The life work of a*Samartha Sadgru* (Perfect Master) leads one to identify with the redemption of theSupreme Being."16

Among these functions, the function of Protection or Ruling definitely was the most predominant theme or feature of Sri Shirdi Sai Baba's Avatarhood. Therefore, He was undoubtedly Shiva's *avatar.* It is on record that when the Fakir Patil's wife Fakiri was carrying Babu(child Baba) to Guru Venkusha's Ashram at Sailu, Venkusha had a dream the previous night in which Lord Shiva had appeared before him and told him thatHe himself would be coming to his Ashram at 11:00 a.m. the next day.

Sri Shirdi Sai Baba As Avatar Of Lord Dattatreya

Sri Shirdi Sai Baba appeared in the form of a three-headed divine childDattatreya before a group of his devoteeson Dattatreya Jayanti in 1911, andBalwant C. Kohojkar had himself witnessed this miraculous revelation. This has been evidenced by his son Sanker Balwant Kohojkar's testimony.17

Sri Shirdi Sai Baba As The Supreme One (All Gods And Goddesses RolledInto One)

All the above clues to the reality of Sri Sai Baba are undoubtedly true but truerthan all these was what He himself had declared and what was revealed throughhis behaviour pattern and actions. He had declared this about Himself:

"I am not confined within this body of 3 ½ cubits-height; I am everywhere; see me in every place".18

"People think they are all different from each other. But in this, they are wrong. I am inside you. You are inside me."19

"I am the Inner Ruler of all hearts and seated in their hearts."

"I am the Controller – the wirepuller of the show of this Universe."

"I am omnipresent, occupying land, air, country, world, light and heaven and that I am not limited."

"I am the mother – origin of all senses, the Creator, Preserver and Destroyer.

Nothing will harm him who turns his attention towards Me, but Maya will lash or whip him who forgets Me. All the insects, ants, the visible, movable and immovable world are in my Body or Form.20

Thus he had declared to be the Supreme Being, the Almighty God, who hasbeen and is still being worshipped in numerous forms of Gods, Goddesses,Prophets, Saints and Masters in different religions throughout the world. Not only did He profess as such but He actually demonstrated this very convinginglywith transparent sincerity and honesty before all those who saw Him, lived withHim, visited Him and became His devotees. Although, He was a Brahmin, he never tried to assert this fact. Although, He was aware of his parentage and placeand circumstances of birth, He did not want to disclose this to the people asHe did not want to have any worldly links with his relatives or people of Pathri village. Although He was Himself God incarnate – *Ishwara, Allah* or *Bhagavan*,instead of asserting this fact, He usually described Himself as *fakir* or *Allah*'sservant. He used to say, *Allah Malik hai* (God is the Master), thus implying thatHe himself was merely a servant of God who carried out *Allah*'s orders or wishes.The following factual portrayal of Sri Shirdi Sai Baba as presented in *ShriSai Sat Charita* very clearly reveals his identity as a unique universal saintwho had genuine regard and concern for the saints and followers of all other religions, and who in turn was the recipient of great adoration, love and worship of the saints and followers of other religions of his times:

"Let us see what sort of personage was Sai Baba. He conquered this *samsar* (worldlyexistence) which is very difficult and hard to cross. Peace or mental calm was hisornament. He was the home of Vaishnav devotees, most liberal (like Karna)amongst liberals, the quintessence of all essences. He had no love for perishablethings and was always engrossed in self-realization. He felt no pleasure in the thingsof the world or of the world beyond. His *antarang* (heart) was as clear as a mirrorand his speech like nectar. The rich and the poor were the same for him. He didnot know or care for honour or dishonour. He was the Lord of all beings. He spokefreely and mixed with all people, saw the acting and dances of dancing girls and heard *gazal* songs. Still He swerved not an inch from *samadhi* (mental equilibrium).The name of *Allah* was always on his lips. While the world awoke, he slept andwhile the world slept, He was vigilant."21

"....If you think that He was a Hindu, He looked like a *Yavan* (Muslim). If youthink him to be a *Yavan,* He looked like a pious Hindu. No one definitely knewwhether He was a Hindu or a Mohammedan. He celebrated the Hindu festival of Rama-Navami with all due formalities and at the same time permitted the *'sandal'*procession of the Mohammedans. ...If you call Him Hindu, He always lived inthe masjid; if Mohammedan, He always had the *dhuni,* (the sacred fire) and the following things which are contrary to Mohammedan religion, i.e., grinding on th e*chakki* handmill, blowing of the *sankh*(conch), ringing bells, oblation in the fire, *bhajan,* givingof food and worshipping of Baba's feet by means of *arghya* (water) were alwaysallowed there. If you think that He was a Mohammedan, the best of Brahmins and *Agnihotris,* leaving aside their orthodox ways, fell prostrate at his feet. Sai Baba wassuch a saint, who saw no difference between caste and creed and even beings andbeings. He took meat and fish with Fakirs, but did not grumble when dogs touchedthe dishes with their mouth. ...How could He, who even in dreams never warded off cats and dogs by harsh words and signs, refuse food to poor and helpless people.He saw divinity in all beings. Friends and foes were alike to Him. He even obliged the evil doer and was the same in prosperity and adversity. No doubt ever touchedHim."22

Thus we can see that Sri Shirdi Sai Baba was indeed a unique saint.

The Galaxy of Sri Shirdi Sai Baba's Contemporary Saints

There were 54 or 56 saints who were the contemporaries of Sri Shirdi Sai Baba and were in contact with Him in some way or the other and about whom Ihave been able to discover some valuable information from Sai Literature and other spiritual literature of his times.

Before I briefly highlight about them, the following interesting points may be noted:

(1) Not only in his life as Sai Baba of Shirdi in the 19th-20th centuries, but even in a number of his previous births, he had been a Saint. It may be

recalled that he was as incarnation of Dattatreya, He was Kabir, He was that *Fakir* who had assured the distressed ruler of India, Humayun, that a son would be born to him at Uramakot and he would be the emperor of the country and He had met the great Hindu spiritualist of Kashi Mukund (who incarnated as Emperor Akbar); he had been leading saintly lives at different periods of time.

(2)   The very circumstances of his birth and upbringing reveal that allound him there were saints or saintly people. His father Ganga Bhavadia had already decided to become a *sanyasi* and had actually left his house. His motherDevagiriamma also had decided to become a renunciate and follow her husbandto the forest. His father did not even wait for her delivery in the forest and went away in utter *vairagya*, leaving Devagiriamma all alone in the forest where she delivered the child. She also abandoned he child in the forest soon after thebirth and went following her renunciate husband's footsteps. Then, Muslim fakir Patil and his wife *Fakiri* found the newborn baby. They took it with them to theirhouse at Manwat and brought him up. They named the child "Babu". Thus inHis childhood itself Baba was cultivated into *fakiri* (mode of beggar saint or mendicant).

(3)   The formative influences of the Brahmin Guru Venkusha and his *ashram* at Sailu for twelve years on Babu from his age of 4 to 16, were most significant. The *Guru* moulded him into the mould of the unique saint that he emerged by his teachings, blessings and bestowal of special grace or powers.Sri Shirdi Sai Baba duly acknowledged the greatness of His Guru Venkusha and the deep debt He owed to him for all the matchless love and grace that heshowered on him. Besides, Guru Venkusha, the influence of His peer group in the *ashram* also had its effect. Babu (adolescent Baba) served his teacher withtotal devotion and utmost love and Guru Venkusha, in turn loved him most.This had caused jealousy in the hearts of a number of boys who were all thetime trying to browbeat him and ultimately one day they overpowered and hithim with a brick on his forehead in the forest. Baba did not harbour any ill will whatsoever against his peers even in such circumstances. Baba had a close friend Sakha Ram in the Guru Venkusha ashram at Sailu, who later became famous as Sakha Ram Maharaj, the great saint of Angaon Kawas. Baba and Sakha Ram maintained cordial links for several decades, though Sakha Ram Maharaj never came to Shirdi. Sri Sai Baba of Shirdi had,

of course, miraculously manifestedHimself at Sakha Ram's place many times.

(4) After leaving his Guru's *ashram* in 1854, Babu, the young boy saint reached Shirdi, stayed there for barely two months and then wandered fromplace to place. During this time, for some years He stayed in a mosque at Aurangabad where He instructed a Muslim Faqir Peer Mohammed, who latercame to Shirdi and stayed with Baba during 1909-1918 and was known as *'BadeBaba'* who was given Rs. 90 per day by Baba for many years our of the *dakshina* received by him from devotees. Baba lived with another Fakir, Ali (perhaps Akbar Ali) in a mosque in Ahmednagar for some time. Baba once spoke about an old Muslim Fakir whom He had served by begging alms and food for him daily for some time. In all probability, he was Bade Baba as mentioned above,but it is also ossible that there might have been some other saint whom Baba had served. SaiBaba must have met a number of Hindu and Muslim saints during his wanderings during 1852-58 and thus he might have assimilated thecharacteristics of both Hindu and Muslim saints which formed his compositeand universalistic personality.

(5) Baba reached Shirdi for the second time in 1858 and stayed therepermanently till his *Mahasamadhi* on October 15, 1918. In this long spanof six decades, many saints came to Shirdi to seek His *darshan* and blessings.Among them were such great saints as Gadge Maharaj, Alindi Swami, DarveshShah, Maddu Shah, Bal Gangadhar Tilak, etc. Many saints, who in their hearts of hearts, or through their intuition knew that Sri Shirdi Sai Baba was then the greatest spiritual power on earth, and had sent their devotees to seek the their devotees to seek the *darshan* and blessings of the great Master. Among them were such great spiritual luminaries as Anandswami, Yogi Kulkarni, Tembe Maharaj, Narsing Maharaj,Ramanand Bidkar Maharaj, Vaman Shashi Islampurkar, etc. A number of saints never visited Shirdi and also Baba never visited them at their Ashrams, *mutts* orplaces physically and none of them sent his disciples to Baba and *vice versa*. But those saints were in constant contact with Baba internally. Among such saints,mention may be made of Tajuddin Baba, Sakha Ram Maharaj, Dhuniwale Dada, Vishnudevanand Saraswati, Banne Mia, Shamsuddin Fakir, Bannu Mai,Baba Jan, etc. Baba himself sent his messages, gifts and blessings to some saintslike

Banne Mia and Shamsuddin Fakir. Then there were a number of saints likeRaman Maharishi, Akkalkot Swami, Guru Gholap etc. who had such invisibleyet deep spiritual identification with Baba that Baba appeared in the form of these saints to their devotees when they visited Shirdi and looked at Baba orHis photograph placed in Gurusthan. It may also be recalled that yet another category of saints drawn to Baba were his devotees, who later on grew up ass due to Baba's grace, guidance and divine help; although they were youngor middle aged devotees but later on they became famous.

(6) Baba had made two declarations about himself:

"I do not instruct through the ear (I do not give any *mantra),* our traditions are different".

"I have no disciples in this world, I have countless devotees. You do not recognize the distinction between a disciple and a devotee. Any one can be a devotee, butthat is not the case with the disciple. ... A disciple is one who carries out implicitly the commands of Guru. The mark of the *shishya* is total devotion to the *preceptor*(Guru). One the man who says, I have none in the world other than the preceptoris a disciple." Yet, some of his devotees greatly benefited from Baba's spiritual contact andbecame great saints in due course of time Upasani Maharaj became an eminentsaint mainly due to Baba's training. Mention ought to be made of Abdul Baba, Das Ganu, Sai Sharan Anand, Megha, Bhisma, Mhalasapati, Shivamma Thayee, Hemadpant, Mathaji Krishnapriya and some others who belong to this privileged category of Sai Baba's contemporary saints – the devotee – saints.

Nows brief and essential information about fifty-four saints, which could be available to me in the whole of Sai literature. They werethe contemporaries of Sri Shirdi Sai Baba and had contacts with Him in someway or the other.

Sri Sai Baba's Contemporary Saints

(1) Fakir Patil: Muslim fakir of Manwat ; Years of Contact with Baba during1835-39.He was the Sufi Fakir who brought up child Baba, named him 'Babu', wasa loving and pious Fakir. Differences of creed, caste and race did not exist In hismind; the Initial training and loving care by him in Baba's childhood cast themould of the *fakiri* (ascetism) of Sai Baba.

(2) Guru Venkusha: Hindu Brahman Saint of Sailu; Years of contact with Babaduring 1839-51.

He was a rich landlord of Sailu turned Into a saint; started *ashram* for orphanand helpless boysin hisbighpltizl house;he was a great devotee of Lord Venkateswara;he identified himself with God in the form of Venkatesha and assumed the nameof Venkusha; saint of very broad and universal values; loved Babu most;h gave the brick and a *chadar* cloth to Babu at the time of his departure from his *ashram* in1854.

(3) Sakha Ram Maharaj: Hindu of Sailu & Angaonkava; peer of Baba during1839-51. Baba's *Gurubhai* (classmate) under Guru Venkusha, had much love andfriendship with Baba; Baba visited Sakha Ram Maharaj's Mutt at Angaonkavaand they both planted two mango saplings; young Baba often materialisedhimself near his place near Angaonkava.

(4) Bade Baba: Muslim Fakir of Aurangabad, Years of contact with Baba around1853-54, 1857 & 1909-1918. Baba instructed him in a mosque in Paithan,Aurangabad for some years; Baba again visited him there; he came to stay withBaba in 1909. Baba used to give him Rs. 90 per day out of His daily *dakshina*collections.

(5) Ali (Akbar Ali): Muslim of Ahmad Nagar, Around 1855-57.Baba lived with him in a mosque for some time. A photograph of Ali andBaba was found in the family of Seth of Rahata village.

(6) Gadge Maharaj: Hindu (Parit: washerman) Shivagaon Around early1858-1918.Baba came to his village and asked him for *roti,* which he gave. He came tomeet Baba before his *Maha Nirvana* and was greeted with abuses and blessingsby Baba.

(7) Devidas: Hindu; Shirdi; 1858-80 or so. He came to Shirdi before Baba in1846; Baba liked him and often lived with him in Maruti temple and *Chavdi* for some time.

(8) Jankidas: Hindu, Shirdi, 1862-75. He came to Shirdi and settled there; Babaand he often met and talked on spiritual matter.

(9) Akkalkot Swami: Hindu, Akkalkot, 1878. At the time of his *Maha Nirvana*he told his disciple Keshav Naik that he would manifest as Sai Baba of Shirdi.He was a great Master.

(10) Anand Swami: Hindu, Yevala Mutt, 1885. On seeing Baba on his first visit to Shirdi, he said, "He (Baba) is a diamond.

(11) Faqir Aminuddin: Muslim, Nanded, 1889. Baba appeared in a dreamto him and asked him to send his servant Abdul to Shirdi as Baba's personalattendant.

(12) Gangagir Bua: Hindu, Puntambe 1896. He told Nana Saheb Dengle thatSai Baba was a *Chintamani* (gem) on his first visit to Shirdi; visited Baba often.

(13) Guru Datta: Hindu, Gangapur, 1908.A great Guru and Tantrik; he taughtKhusha Bhai to materialize sweets etc. He directed Khusha Bhai to go to "Myelder brother Sai Baba" and do whatever he directed.

(14) Tembe Swami: Hindu, 1909. In 1909 he told Sagun Meru Naik of Goathat Baba was a man of *great darbar*; Naik came to Sai Baba in 1912, settled at Shirdi and started his hotel serving Baba's devotees.

(15) Durvesh Shah: Muslim; Aurangabad; 1910. He directed Imambhai Chote Khan of Vajapur to go to Sai Baba to seek his grace in the matter of litigation with his mother-in-law and gave him all the directions on how to approach Sai Baba politely and seek his grace.

(16) Vijayananda Swami: Hindu, 1910. He came to see Baba and duly receivedhis grace.

(17) Narayan Maharaj: Hindu, Khedagaon, 1911. He had directed Kashinath Upasani to go to Sai Baba.

(18) Siddharood Maharaj: Hindu, Hubli, 1911. Sagun Meru Naik came to Babafrom Siddharood Maharaj. Baba told him "You have come from Mota Darbar"(a great saint's court).

(19) Yogi Kulkarni: Hindu, Rahuri, 1911. He directed Kashi Nath Upasani togo to see Sai Baba at Shirdi saying "He was a great *Aulia* (Saint)."

(20) Durvesh Saheb: Muslim, 1911. He stayed with Baba for some days and wascordially treated by Baba.

(21) Ramanand Bidkar Maharaj: Hindu, 1912. He told his disciple Khandu Rao Gadre to go to Sai Baba and prophesied that Baba would address him as 'Ramdas'.

(22) Narayan Asram: Hindu, Vaman Mutt, Gangapuri Wai, 1914. Baba gave him the first push towards spirituality and service.

(23) Narsing Maharaj: Hindu, Nasik, 1916. He sent his disciple Hansraj toBaba, saying that Baba would give him two slaps on the face and that

wouldremove the evil spirit which had been preventing him from having progeny. He and Baba were constantly aware of what either of them was doing at his place.

(24) B.G.Tilak: Hindu, Pune, 1917. Famous politician, nationalist and religiousscholar; first visited Baba at Shirdi on May 19, 1917.

(25) Shamsuddin Mia Faqir: Muslim, Fakir Aurangabad, 1918. Baba sent him meat and Rs. 250 to do *moulu, Kawali* and *Nyas* ceremonies, predicting Hispassing away in the next few months. He must have been very close to Babainwardly.

(26) Banne Mia Faqir: Muslim, Aurangabad, 1918. Baba sent him a garland of*sevenththi* flowers and message *Nav Din Nav Tarikh Allah Mia Apna Dhunia lejayenge Marji Allakhi* conveying the exact date of his coming *Maha Nirvan*.

(27) Alindi Swami: Hindu, Alindi. Came to Baba; Baba relieved him of severe ear pain just by His blessings.

(28) Baba Jaan: (Lady Saint) Muslim, Saint Pune. She kissed Meher Baba when he was a young boy on his forehead and prophesied that he would become a great *Avatar*

(29) Baba Tajuddin: Muslim, Saint of Nagpur. A great Saint (Perfect Master); had spiritual contact with Baba. A lot of information is available on him on theinternet.

(30) Bannu Mayi: Muslim, Bhodegaon. A 20 year old unmarried lady Saint inhighly advanced spiritual state, roamed like a mad naked saint In jungle; Baba's devotee Nana Chandorkar could trace her and offer worship and his gifts to herbecause of Baba's miraculous divine Instructions to that saint.

(31) Bhapkar Maharaj: Hindu. Baba welcomed his son and got him worshippedlike himself in *Dwarkamai* out of His regard for his pious and learned father.

(32) Daji Maharaj: Hindu (Brahmin).Baba referred to him as His brother; Baba appeared in the form of Maruti in his Ashram.

(34) Dhoonivale Dada: Hindu Sai Kheda in 1987 (Took *Mahasamadhi)* atKhandwa. He had spiritual contact with Baba. Baba appeared in the dream of Sadashiv of Harda to say, "Now I am at Sai Kheda (as Dhoonivale Dada),Come for my *darshan* here", after Baba's *Maha Nirvana* in 1918. He was a great *Avadhoot* (Perfect Master).

(35) Hilda Beg: Muslim, Kanad (Near Aurangabad). Came to Baba; Baba directed him to change his name to *Panja Shah* and to settle down at the Cantonment near Kanad where he was later treated as a saint.

(36) Madhu Shah: Muslim Meran Jalgaon. He came to seek Rs. 700 as helpfrom Baba for building a mosque.

(37) Madhav Nath: Hindu. He sent his disciple Bhau Pradhan to seek Baba's blessing for the ear-piercing ceremony and ask whether a gold nail should be putin the earhole. Before he could ask, Baba told him that a gold nail should be putin the earhole.

(38) Ramana Maharishi: Hindu, Godman, Tiruvannmalai. Sai Baba gave *darshan* as Raman Maharishi to the latter's disciple Mrs. Dongre (photographkept at Gurusthan, Shirdi on 3.3.1953).

(39) Somdeva Swami: Hindu, Haridwar (U.P.). He had to face Baba's anger because of his having doubts on Baba's spirituality after seeing Baba's grandparaphernalia of flag, decoration etc.; later on became Baba's staunch devotee.

(40) Vaman Shasi: Muslim, Islampurkar. He was Guru of Das Ganu whoapproved of Das Ganu's going to meet Baba; he also stayed with Baba for three days.

(41) Vishdevanand Saraswati: (Alias Tembe Maharaj) Hindu, Narmada. He hadspiritual contact with Baba. He sent a coconut to Baba through Das.

(42) Mhalasapathy Hindu, Shirdi.(Born on 11.9.22) Sunar (Goldsmith) Caste;Priest of Khandoba Temple). In 1858; he gave the name 'Sai' to Baba; was the constant companion and ardent worshipper of Baba during 1858-1918.

(43) Abdul Baba: Muslim Nanded 1889. (Born in 1879 or so). He was sent by his earlier Master Fakir Aminuddin to Baba to serve Him; lived with Babatill the end; did all menial jobs like cleaning the mosque, street, Baba's clothes,filling water in masjid pots, lighting lamps etc. Baba instructed and trainedhim into a Fakir and spiritual saint. Baba revealed to him that in His nextincarnation when He would be known as 'Sathya'.

(44) Das Ganu: Hindu(Brahmin)Akolner1890.(Ganpatrao Dattatreya Sahashrabuddhe, Police Constable). He first met Baba in 1890; took Nana Saheb Chandorkar to Baba; resigned from Police service in 1903 on Baba'spersistent advice, and started singing *kirtans* of Baba; composed a

number ofprayers and poems on Baba; led Urs-Ram Navmi yearly kirtans at Shirdi underBaba from 1914; became a great saint of Pandarpur.

(45) Nana N.G. Chandorkar: Hindu, Brahmin (1890).(Deputy Collector). He was brought to Baba by Das Ganu in 1890; was a scholarly spiritual seeker;discussed many spiritual matters with Baba and received many miraculous graces from Him; rendered great service to Baba; was always privileged to sit near Baba while most of the devotees had to stand before Him.

(46) Shama: Hindu, (Brahmin) Shirdi. He was a teacher in the Government Primary School in Shirdi which adjoined Baba's masjid; became Baba'sclose devotee; Baba sent him as his representative to other's homes on many occasions; was a witness to most of the *leelas,* miracles and talks of Babathroughout His life.

(47) Radha Krishana Ayi (*Mayi*): Hindu (Brahmin). A young devoted widowwho came to Shirdi to serve Baba by cleaning Masjid, street, etc. looked after the devotees; was a strict disciplinarian, hot tempered lady; her house was called "School for Sai devotees." Baba sent many visitors and devotees to her forlearning spiritual secrets Inherent in her service and wisdom. Her house waa a sort of spitual school for Ba ba's new visitors.

(48) G.S. Kharpade: Hindu, 1909.(Ganesh Srikrishna) (Advocate & MLC). First met Baba on December 5,1909;also visited In 1910 and many times thereafter; Baba revealed *rinanubandha* (ties of many previous births) with himand his wife. His *'Shirdi Diary'* gives Intimate daily account of Baba's moods and miracles during the 1910's.

(49) Anna Saheb Dabholkar: Hindu (Brahmin)(Govind Rao Raghavnath) (1856-1929) (Resident Magistrate). Born in a poor family; a self-made man,started career as a clerk and rose to became Magistrate; First met Baba in 1990;became his ardent devotee. Baba conferred on him the title 'Hemadpant';permitted him to write His biography *Shri Sai Sat Charita* in Marati; he greatlyhelped Baba's *Sansthan* till his death in 1929

(50) Upasani Maharaj: Hindu (Brahmin), 1914.(Kashinath Upasani), (Life span15.5.1870 to 24.12.1941). an earnest spiritual seeker; met Baba on June 1911;Baba trained him in spirituality; he slipped away from Shirdi in the midnightof 25.7.1914, lectured in Scinde, Nagpur and Kharagpur; established *Kanya Kumari Sansthan* at Sakori near Shirdi for training *kanyas* for the performanceof *Yagnas* and other intricate Vedic rituals and

spreading spirituality through women.A lot of information about him and his Sakori *ashram* is available on theinternet.

(51) Shivamma Thayee: Hindu, Pallachi, 1906-1918.(Original name Rajamma Gounder (Coimbatore).(Life span 16.5.1891 to 7.7.1994). She first saw Sai Baba at Pallachi near Coimbatore as a 15 years old married girl; Baba gave her *Gayatri mantra* writing it in Tamil; visited Baba 5-6 times at Shirdi till 1917;she witnessedo some of the Baba's yogic miracles; Baba changed her name to Shirvamma in 1917 and directed to her to go to Banglore. My book *"My Life With Sri Shirdi Sai Baba'* presents my detailed intrrvire with her.

(52) Sri Sharan Anandji: Hindu (Brahmin).(Sri Wamenbhai Pran Govind Patel)Gujarat.Bardoli (Gujrat) Visited Baba in 1911 and 1913-14. Blessed by Baba; wrotebooks on Baba; in 1959 assumed the name of Sri Sharanand and took *sanyas;*He inaugurated the statue of Sai Baba in Baba's Samadhi Temple in 1952.

(53) Meher Baba: Parsi, Pune,. Visited Sai Baba in 1915 as young boy;Baba addresses as *"Parvar Digar"* (God). was directed by Baba to go to Upasani Baba.Became a great saint. A lot of information on him as available in,Yogi M.K.Spencer;s book *'How I Found God'* and on the intrnet.

(54) Sai Narayan Baba: Hindu, Krishnapure 1914 (Born on February 2, 1911) near Udipi (Karnataka). Stayed in Ganegapur (AP) and then in Sanjeeva RaddynNagar, Secunderabad.In 1914 on Diwali day, he was kidnapped as a 3 ½ years old child, stripped of all ornaments and left on a Bombay-bound train, at Dhond station he was noticed by a group of Sai Baba devotees who took him to Shirdi; Baba addressedhim "Lo, my child you have come, I have been waiting for you, "He told Hisdevotees that the child Narayan would be a *Mahapurush* (Great saint); stayed with Baba till 1918; then with Abdul for two years; acquired powers to materialisehot *udi* (holy ash) and cure people. He spread Baba's name in the world.

AnalysisA close perusal and analysis of the above date on Sri Sai Baba's contemporaryfifty-four saints reveals the following interesting facts:

(1) Out of the 54 saints mentioned above, 13 were Muslims, 1 Parsi and40 Hindus belonging to all castes but mostly to the Brahmin caste and, some lower castes and some were *Sanyasis*. This shows that there existed

a free-flowing interaction and cordiality between Sri Shirdi Sai Baba and the contemporarysaints of different religions and castes.

(2) Sri Shirdi Sai Baba was treated by them as the greatest among them –their Spiritual monitor, leader or guide.

(3) Since Sai Baba was well-versed in both Hindu and Muslim religiousbeliefs, modes of worship and practices and had equal respect for them,the saints of both these religions felt at ease with Him and mixed with Himunhesitatingly. Only some of the fundamentalists among the Muslims did notlike to associate with Him, but they too grudgingly acknowledged his greatnessas an *Auliya* (God man).

(4) In one of his previous incarnations as Kabir, he was an iconoclast who ridiculed most mercilessly the diehard religious rituals and fossilized beliefs of the Hindus and Muslims, but in his incarnation as Sri Shirdi Sai Baba he did not reply the role style of Kabir. Although he sometimes sang Kabir's songs andalso encouraged others to sing hem (even now Kabir's songs are sung with greatgusto in Baba's *Chawdi* at Shirdi by his devotees), yet Baba really respected thetraditional beliefs and modes of worship of both really respected the traditionalbeliefs and modes of worship of both the Hindus and Muslims. He respectedtheir religious symbols, Gods, Goddesses, heroes, festivals and sentiments,and tried His best to show by his personal example how one should follow hisown religion but at the same time fully tolerate and respect other religions.He was against conversion into other religions, and ridiculed it by saying that "It is like changing one's father." He encouraged the reading of Hindu as wellas Muslim scriptures in his *Dwarkamai* Mosque. He lived like a unique saintdeeply immersed in spirituality and genuinely concerned for the physicalwelfare as well as spiritual upliftment and salvation of people of all religionsand also of other creatures. That is why, He had his following among saintsand thousands of people of all religions and also of other creatures. That is why,He had his following among saints and thousands of people of all religions ofcentral and southern regions of India in his lifetime and after his *Maha Nirvan* (passing away) His following has been spreading not only all over India but even in foreigncountries, among Christians, Muslims, Parsis, Hindus, Sikhs, Jains and others.Now He is being worshipped as the most matchless and greatest UniversalMaster of the modern period.

(5) The social and spiritual contacts between Sri Shirdi Sai Baba and thefifty-four saints of his time, highlighted above, clearly project a rare example ofreligious integration, secularism and co-existence created by Sri Sai Baba. Such an example is indeed unprecedented in the annals of the history of human civilisation. What *Bhakti* period saints like Kabir, Nanak, Ravidas, Tulsidas,Mira, etc. were trying to imagine as an ideal way of projection to the masses was actually translated into practice by Sri Shirdi Sai Baba and the galaxy of saints of his time.

(6) How much regard those saints had for Sri Sai Baba and how muchregard Sri Sai Baba had for them is clear from the numerous examples highlighted in the details as to how these saints met Baba often, sent theirdisciples and the messages of cordiality through them. In India today, we find a different picture. There are a number of saints – *Yogis, Swamis, Avatars,Mahants, Achryas, Fakirs,* Godmen or *Gurus.* Many of them do not see eye toeye, and in their discourses and writings they do not feel shy in giving vent totheir mutual jealousies and their tendency to slight or belittle other saints. Todaymany of them have close links with politicians, rich people, fundamentalistelements and *tantriks* and are seen hankering after money, power, *ashrams,*publicity, properties and all such manifestations of *maya.* It is in this contextthat we can very clearly understand and appreciate the greatness, beauty andgrandeur of the unique example of the spirituality par excellence and secularismof the highest order reflected by the galaxy of the contemporary saints of SriShirdi Sai Baba.

(7) During Sri Shrdi Sai Baba's life time (1838-1918), there were a numberof other nationallyand internationallyknown saintslike Sri RamakrishnaParamhansa, Vivekananda, Sri Aurobindo, Sri Ramana Maharishi, Sri Mother of Pondicherry, Sant Kripal Singh, Sri Devaraha Baba, Sri Lahiri Mahasya, Sri Yogananda Paramhamsa, Anandmayee Ma etc. It is worth noting that there is nomention of Sri Shirdi Sai Baba in the writings by, or about any of these saints, of their meting or contact with Sri Shirdi Sai Baba.This is indeed surprising but not disturbing. The Editorial of *Shri Sai Leela*(May, 1983) gives us a valuable guidance. It says, "Great Minds Think Alike".It rightly points that all those saints working on the same wavelength had emphasised virtually the same things – unity in diversity, religious toleration,morality and concern for spiritual elevation.Taking the examples of Swami Vivekanand to illustrate this point, the Editorial has rightly mentioned the following:

"It is quite interesting to note here how the minds of the great people are thinking alike. Swami Vivekanand was never known to have visited Shirdi, nor Sai Baba had any open discussion with Swamiji in His lifetime, still the thoughts about religion expressed by both these saints are quite alike. The tensions between the Hindus and Muslims, in particular, were rising in India and the basic principles of all religions being more or less the same, the great thinkers of the world have always been thinking why there should at all be a conflict among the religions of the world. The prophets or saints who started a religion always had the thought of the people before them. They had to think of that which would hold the society together.".…The unrest in the world was properly analysed by great thinkers like Sri Sai Baba and Swami Vivekanand and they had come to the conclusion that itwas no use trying to destroy or overpower any of the established religions inthe world. The only solution to end the religious conflict is tolerance. Every staunch follower of any religion should learn to honour other man's religion.It is necessary for every one to understand the good principles of other religionsand to inculcate them in one's mind. Swami Vivekananda has, therefore, ruled out the conversion of one person from one religion to another and he, thereforesays, "Every person should preserve his speciality and grasping the essence ofother religions, he should develop his personality and prosper according to hisown individuality. Sri Sai Baba as also expressed similar thoughts on several occasions while dealing with persons professing different religions.Though apparently one wonders as to how great minds think in the same direction, really speaking there is no reason for any sort of wonder in this respect. The spiritual level of all great thinkers and saint os so high that theyare communicating with each other without any visible media. …From *'Shri SaiSat Charita'* we can cite several examples to show that there is a communionamong the saints even through they may be far away from each other withoutany difficulty."

References and Notes

1. Bhardwaja, *Sai Baba The Master,* p.77.
2. *Gita.*
3. Briggs, George Weston, *Gorakhnath and the Kanphatta Yogis.* Delhi: Motilal Banarsi Das, 1973, pp. 1-2.

4. Rajneesh, *Sat Guru Mile Ta Ubre (Gorakh-vani)*. Delhi: Diamond Pocket Books, 1991, p. 95 (in Hindi).

5. *Ibid.,* p. 95.

6. Macauliffe, Max Arthur, *The Sikh Religion, Its Gurus, Sacred Writings and Authors.* Combridge: Oxford, 1909, Voll, p. 225.

7. *Bhavan's Journal* (Bhartiya Vidhya Bhavan, Bombay), Vol. XXIV, No. 6, October 23, 1977, p. 23. (Special issue devoted to Paramhansa Yogananda).

8. Goyandka, Jayadayal, *Param Sadhan.* Gorakhpur; Gita Press, p. 304. (In Hindi).

9. Rajneesh, *Jas Panihar Dhare Sir Gagar* (in Hindi). Pune: Rajneesh Foundation, 1991, pp.67.

10. Gunaji, *Shri Sat Charita,* p. xxiii.

11. White, "The Sai Baba Movement: Approaches to the Study of Indian Saints", *The Journal of Asian Studies,* Vol. XXXI, No. 4, August 1972, pp. 863-878.

12. Aiyer, *Perfect Master,* p. 2.

13. Aiyer, *Ibid.,* p. 3.

14. Bhardwaja, *Op. Cit.,* p. 297.

15. Sri Sathya Sai Baba's revelations in:
    (i) Sandweiss, *Sai Baba and the Psychiatrist.*
    (ii) Murthy, *The Life and Teachings of Sri Sai Baba of Shirdi,* 1974.

16. Narasimhaswamiji, *The Wondrous Saint Sai Baba,* (VI Edition), p. 103.

17. (i) Narasimhaswamiji, (Ed.) *Devotees' Experiences of Sri Sai Baba,* p.
    (ii) *Ibid.,* p.199.
    (iii) The Shirdi Sai Saga: Mystery and Miracles, *Sanathana Sarathi,* November, 1992, p. 258.

18. *Devotees' Experiences of Sri Sai Baba, Op. Cit.,* p. 82.

19. *Ibid.,* p. 75 (Footnote).

20. *Shri Sai Sat Charita.*

21. *Ibid.,* p. 38.

22. *Ibid.,* p. 60.

References on the Saints: For Further Study

1. Abdul Baba
    Kamath and Kher, *Sri Sai Baba of Shirdi,* pp. 8, 40-41, 93, 192.

2. Akkalkot Maharaj
    (i) Bharadwaja, E., *The Supreme Master: Sri Akkalkot Maharaj.*
    Vidhyarager: Author, 1973.
    (ii) Bharadwaja, *Op. Cit.,* pp. 35, 105-107, 346.
    (iii) Kamath & Kher, *Op. Cit.,* pp. 7, 121-123, 264, 284.
    (iv) Tripathi, A.P., 'Swami Samarth Akkalkot' *Shri Sai Lila,* January,
    1993, pp. 50-53 (In Hindi). Ali (Akbar Ali).

3. Appa (Kannad)
    (i) Bhardwaja, *Op. Cit.,* p. 18.
    (ii) *Shri Sai Leela,* May, 1983, p.6.
    (iii) *Shri Sai Sat Charita,* p. 112.

4. Aminuddin, Faqir
    Kamath & Kher, *Op. Cit.,* pp. 8, 93.

5. Anandswamim: Bharadwaja, *Op. Cit.,* p. 34.

6. Baba Jaan:
    (i) Aiyer, *Op. Cit.,* pp. 264-265.
    (ii) Bhardwaja, *Op. Cit.,* pp. 264-265.

7. Banne Mia Fakir:
    (i) Kamath & Kher, *Op. Cit.,* p. 291.
    (ii) *Devotees' Experiences of Sri Sai Baba,* p. 277.

8. Bannu Mai: Narasinmhasawamiji, *The Wondrous Saint Sai Baba,* pp.
    34-36.

9. Bade Baba (Bade Mia or Malegaon Baba):
    (i) Bhardawaja, *Op. Cit.,* pp. 172-173.
    (ii) Kamath and Kher, *Op. Cit.,* pp. 6,9,103, 291.
    (iii) Khaparde, *Shirdi Diary,* p.38.

10. Bhapkar Maharaj:
    (i) *Shri Sai Leela,* February 1987, pp. 54-56.
    (ii) *Sri Sai Sat Charita.*

11. Daji Maharaj: *Devotees' Experiences of Sri Sai Baba,* p.62.

12. Das Ganu Maharaj: *Devotees' Experiences of Sri Sai Baba,* pp. 119.
    (ii) *Narasimhaswamiji, Life of Sai Baba,* pp, vi-xi.

13. Devagiriamma: Sri Sathya Sai Baba's Discourse, *Sanathana Sarathi,* November 1990, pp. 294-296.

14. Devidas:
    (i) Bhardwaja, *Op. Cit.,* p. 34.
    (ii) Kamath & Kher, *Op. Cit.,* pp. 7, 79, 103.
    (iii) *Shri Sai Sat Charita.*

15. Dhuniwale Dada:
    (i) Bhardwaja, *Op. Cit.,* p. III.
    (ii) Revanandji Keshvanandji Brahmchari, *Sri Dhunivale Dada Kathmrita.* Ujjain, Rajesh Printers (Two Parts in Hindi).

16. Darvesh Saheb:
    (i) Jaitley, G.K. & Kusum, *Sri Dada Vinay. Dada Chalisa.* Delhi: Jaya Rani Jaitley, 712, Nai Basti, Katra Neel.

17. Darvesh Saheb:
    (i) Bhardwaja, *Op. Cit.,* p. 169.
    (ii) Khaparde, *Op. Cit.,* p.
    (iii) *Devotees' Experiences of Shri Sai Baba,* p. 273.

18. Gadge Maharaj:
    (i) Bhardwaja, *Op. Cit.,* pp. 18-20.
    (ii) Rao, M.R. "Saint Gadge Maharaj" *Shri Sai Lila,* Jan., 1983, p. 53.
    (iii) Guruji, K.G. Vankhade, *Saint Godge Baba,* New Delhi: Publication Division, Govt. of India, 1986. (In Hindi)

19. Gajanan Maharaj
    (i) Kamath & Kher, *Op. Cit.,* p. 154.
    (ii) Tripathi, *Op. Cit.,* pp. 73.

20. Ganga Bhavadia: Sri Sathya Sai Baba's Discourse, *Sanathana Sarathi,* Nov. 1990, pp. 294-296.

21. Gangagir Bua:
    (i) Bhardwaja, *Op. Cit.,* p 34.
    (ii) Kamath & Kher, *Op. Cit.,* pp. 3, 7, 74, 285.

22. Gholap Maharaj: Bharadawaj, *Op. Cit.,* pp. 107-108.

23. Gorakhnath: Briggs, *Op. Cit.*

24. Guru Datta: *Devotees' Experiences of Shri Sai Baba,* pp. 203-205.

25. Hilda Beg: Bhardwaja, *Op. Cit.,* p. 64.

26. Jankidas, Gosavi:
    (i) Bharadwaj, *Op. Cit.*, p. 34.
    (ii) Kamath & Kher, *Op. Cit.*, pp.7, 79.
    (iii) *Shri Sai Sat Charita.*
27. Kabir:
    (i) Kamath & Kher, *Op. Cit.*, pp. 12, 25, 27, 50, 87, 94, 106.
    (ii) Jafri, Sardar, Ali, *Kabir Bani:* Bombay: Hindustani Book Trust, 1965 (In Hindi).
    (iii) Varma, R.K., *Kabir: Biography and Philosophy,* New Delhi: Prints India, 1989 (II Ed.)
28. Kulkarni, Yogi: Bharadawaja, *Op. Cit.*, p. 255.
29. Maddu Shah: *Devotees' Experiences of Shri Sai Baba*, p. 281.
30. Madhavnath: Bharadawaja, *Op. Cit.*, p. 187.
31. Megha:
    (i) Kamath & Kher, *Op. Cit.*, pp. 114-118, 257, 265.
    (ii) Naasimhaswami, *Life of Sai Baba* (Part II), pp.
32. Mehar Baba:
    (i) Aiyer, *Op. Cit.*, pp. 25-32.
    (ii) Narasimhaswamiji, *Life of Sai Baba* (Part II), pp. 1-48.
33. Narsing Maharaj:
    (i) Bharadwaja, *Op. Cit.*, pp. 103-104.
    (ii) *Shri Sai Lila,* May, 1983, p.4.
34. Narayan Asram:
    (i) *Devotees' Experiences of Sri Sai Baba*, pp. 60-63.
    (ii) Narasimhaswamiji, *The Wondrous Saint Sai Baba*, pp. 69-71.
35. Narayan Maharaj: Aiyer, *Op. Cit.*, pp. 21-24.
36. Radha Krishna Ayi:
    (i) Bharadwaja, *Op. Cit.*, pp. 269-70.
    (ii) Kamath & Kher, *Op. Cit.*, p. 269.
37. Patil, Faqir: Sri Sathya Sai Baba's revelation, *Sanathana Sarathi* Nov. 1990, pp. 192.
38. Ramana Mehrishi: Osborne, *The Collected Works of Ramana Maharishi,* Tirvannmalai: Sri Ramansramam, 1974.
39. Ramanand Bidkar Maharaj: Bharadwaja, *Op. Cit.*, p. 128.
40. Sai Narayan Baba: Sri Sai Narayan Baba: Booklet.
41. Sai Sharan Anand:

(i) Bhardwaja, *Op. Cit.*, pp. 41-44.

(ii) *Shri Sai Leela,* November, 1982, pp. 41-44.

42. Sakha Ram Maharaj: Bhardwaja, *Op. Cit.*, p. 24-25.
43. Samsuddin Mia Faqir:

(i) Kamath, & Kher, *Op. Cit.*, p. 292.

(ii) *Devotees' Experiences of Shri Sai Baba.*

44. Shivamma Thayee: *My Life with Sri Shirdi Sai Baba.* Faridabad: Sai Age Publications, 126, Sector 37, 1992. (M.D. Publication, New Delhi, 1995).
45. Siddharood Maharaj; Bharadwaja, *Op. Cit.*, p. 64.
46. Tajuddin Baba:

(i) Aiyer, *Op. Cit.*, pp. 12-17

(ii) Bhardwaja, *Op. Cit.*, pp. 30-31.

(iii) Meshram, A.K. "Baba Tajuddin Auliya", *Manohar Kahaniyan,* February, 1993, pp. 77-80 (In Hindi).

(iv) Desai, Kant, *Baba Tajuddin Auliya* (Parts I-II). Nagpur: Taj Books, 1995. (In Hindi).

47. Tembe Swami:

(i) Bhardwaja, *Op. Cit.*, pp. 72-73.

(ii) *Shri Sai Leela,* May 1983, p. 6.

(iii) *Shri Sai Sat Charita.*

48. Tilak, B.G.:

(i) Kamath & Kher, *Op. Cit.*, pp.9, 66, 73, 286, 287.

(ii) Khaparde, *Op. Cit.*, p.

(iii) Agarwal, R.C., *Constitutional History of India and National Movement.* New Delhi: S. Chand Co., 1978, pp. 256-357.

49. Upasani Maharaj:

(i) Mani, Sahukar, *The Immortal Gurus of Kanya Kumari Sthan,* pp. 9-14.

(ii) Aiyer, *Op. Cit.*, pp. 8-12.

(iii) Bhardwaja, *Op. Cit.*, pp. 262-264.

(iv) Ghandhy, Rusi, P. "Sri Upasani Maharaj and Kanya Kumari Stan of Sakori in *'All India Sai Samaj Souvenir'* 1996.

(v) Narasimhaswamijii. *Life of Sai Baba* (Part II).

50. Venkusha, Guru Gopal Rao Deshmukh: Kamath & Kher, *Op. Cit.*, pp. 24-29, 80.
51. Vijayanand, Sanyasi:

(i) Bhardwaja, *Op. Cit.*, p. 297.

(ii) *Devotees' Experiences of Shri Sai Baba,* p. 273 (Ch. XXXI).

(iii) *Shri Sai Satcharita.*

52. Vishnudevanand Saraswati: Bhardwaja, *Op. Cit.,* p. 64.

53. Yakub Moulvi: Bhardwaja *Op. Cit.,* p. 64.

Chapter – 6

Sri Shirdi Sai Baba's as the *Jagatguru* (Universal Master)

"Do not say of anyone that he is inimical. Who is whose enemy? Do not entertain ill-feeling towards anyone. All are one and the same."

-Sri Shirdi Sai Baba

Sai Baba lived for 60 years at Shirdi during which period, He did not move out physically to any other town or city. He never saw reailway train. He was never seen by anyone reading a book or writing anything; He never signed; He did not give long scholarly discourses on philosophy or spirituality. He did not make anyone His disciple or spiritual heir. Although thousands of people rushed towards Him to seek His divine grace and protection, only a few names of His close devotees, most of whom belonged to Shirdi village, are heard.

How can such a simple and humble *fakir* living in a small mosque be called a 'Universal Master'? In His own days, the villagers of Shirdi and the visitors thereto thought of Him as their local *chamatkari* (miracle maker) *fakir* having extraordinary divine powers. How more and more people in the world during the last nine decades have come to recognize His stature as a great Universal Master is indeed a topic of great importance.

Although He was born a Brahmin, yet He did not consider it worthwhile to make public and emphasize this fact all his life. He kept people ignorant about His caste, community and parental family. He did not choose to take up the propagation of Hindu religion as His life mission. He was in ideal secularist in the best traditions of religious harmony and unity. He treated all religions with equal respect and strove to bring about communal harmony and emotional and cultural integration among the followers of different religions. Only a genuine Universal master such as Sri Sai Baba of Shirdi could bring Hindus, Muslims, Parsees, Christians and followers of other religions to such an ultimate and supreme realization that all are essentially one and that is the very basis of intrinsic unity and integration among all people.

Instead of merely teaching, preaching or forcing the ideals of secularism, communal harmony and integration, He actually lived these ideals and His unique living example as such is the first testimony of His being considered as the 'Universal Master'.

These days, all kinds of religious, political and social leaders profess grand ideals of secularism, communal harmony and national integration, yet everyone knows how weak is the commitment of the most so them to these ideals and what a fragile and pseudo kind of secularism, unity and integration they have been promoting in society. Even the best known among them are at critical times, found to be exposed as the prisoners of their own parochial religious or sectarian beliefs, merely paying lip service to these ideals. They remain parochial Hindu, Muslim, Sikh, Jain, Christian, etc., refusing to come out of the shells of their own religious beliefs or to treat other religions on equal footing. Their tolerance is superficial, not genuine. Which Hindu religious saint or temple would allow Muslims to read the *Quran* in their temple or *ashram*, and which Muslims saint or mosque would allow the Hindus, Christians and others to read their scriptures in their mosques? Only a *Maha Purush*, the Universal Master, of the stature of Sri Shirdi Sai Baba could do so, as He did at His Dwaraka Mai Masjid at Shirdi with such perfect neutrality, poise and ease that has virtually no parallel in the recorded history of human civilization.

Anyone can read '*Shri Sai Sat Charita*', '*Devotees, experiences of Sri Sai Baba*' and Sai sharananad's '*Sri Sai Baba*' (original Marathi edition) – the three most authentic original sources of information about Sri Shirdi Sai Baba. Therein the avid reader will find that Sri Sai Baba never spoke in favor of or against any religion. He was against religious consideration as such, His basic concern was ethics and good conduct as a human being.

The Universal Master Shirdi Sai Baba's overall effort was directed towards developing in His devotee's moral control over their dispositions. All His informal advice and teachings to His devotees and all His thrilling parables, stories, disclosure of people's past lives and all His own life examples were aimed at one supreme goal; that of making men morally clean, inwardly strong and ever ready to face the ups and down of life, the turmoil's of *sansara* or *bhavsagar* with sense of values and belief in the magnanimity of God who is omnipresent, omnipotent and omniscient.

Despite the fact that Shirdi Sai Baba was a divine personality possessing all supernatural powers and *siddhis* and the fact that if He wished He could certainly live, dress, eat and enjoy in a luxurious manner as many of the present day Swamis, Acharyas and *Mathadeeshes*, etc., are doing, he preferred 'affective neutrality' – an utter disregard to the worldly possessions and facilities, showing no interest in the quality of habitation, food, dress, and no yearning to amass wealth for His *ashram* nor any desire to establish institutions or hereditary *gaddi* (seat) and things like these, which have been so current in the religious circles throughout the world.

A close perusal of Sai Baba's teaching and messages clearly reveal that instead of tying to promote the interests of any particular religion or cult or tying to introduce a new school of spirituality or religious philosophy, Shirdi Sai Baba always clearly and purely emphasized universal values like love, truth, unity, egolessness, detachment, commitment, forbearance, humility, help, hospitality, non-possession, service, surrender etc. all the major religions and moral codes of human societies in the world have always been emphasizing these very values and they are, therefore, treated as universal values.

Shirdi Sai Baba's teachings represent a garland of carefully chosen sweetest flowers of morality and spirituality grown in the flowerbeds of different religions. He Himself advised many of His devotees to study religious scriptures like the *Yoga Vashishta, Ramayana, Gita, Bhagavat, Vishnu Sahsranama, Vithal Pothi, Holy Quran* etc; references to them are there in *Shri Sai Sat Charita* and *Devotees Experiences of Sri Sai Baba*. It is also on record that when Bal Gangadhar Tilak's commentary on the *Gita* was presented to Him, instead of letting it be placed at His holy feet He lifted it up and touched His head with it, saying "Such holy books have their rightful place on our forehead, not at Our feet."

As one reads *Shri Sai Sat Charita* and *Devotees Experiences of Sri Sai Baba* page after page, one discovers Shirdi Sai Baba revealing these very spiritual truths of *Yoga Vashistha* to His devotees and visitors in very simple, rural, rustic words of Marathi and Hindustani. Rama was the paragon of virtues, the establisher of prosperities – *Maryada Purushottam*. Shirdi Sai Baba lived those values and extolled them by His living example as also through His direct, short and penetrating words of unornamented and unembellished speech. He advised His devotees to emulate the virtues of Rama and regularly sing *"Raja Ram, Raja Ram"*.

He often referred to the *Gita* while advising His devotees. He emphasized *sharanagati* (total surrender) before one's Guru, which is the most important teaching of the Gita. In *Shri Sai Sat Charita* there is a very direct and concrete reference to it:

Nana Saheb Chandorkar was a good student of *Vedantsa*. He had read the Gita with commentaries and was proud of his knowledge. He fancied that Baba knew nothing of all that or of Sanskrit till Baba one day pricked the bubble. These were the days before crowds flocked to Baba, when Baba had solitary talks sat the mosques with the devotees. Nana was always sitting near Baba and massaging His legs and muttering something.

> Baba – Nana, what are you mumbling to yourself?
> Nana – I am reciting a *shloka* from Sanskrit.
> Baba – What *shloka*?
> Nana – From the *Bhagavat Gita.*
> Baba – Utter it loudly.
> Nana then recited the *Bhagavat Gita* (IC-34) which is as follows:
> *"Tadviddhi pranipatena pariprashnena sevaya.*
> *Upadeshyanto te jnanam haniastatwwaderashinah."*
> Baba – Nana do you understand it?
> Nana – Yes.
> Baba – If you do, tell Me.
> Nana – It means this-

'Making *sasthanga namaskar*, i.e., prostration, questioning the *guru*, serving Him, learn what this *gyana* is. Then, those *jnanis* who have attained real knowledge of the *Sad-Vastu* (Brahma) will give you *upadesha* (instruction) of *jnana*.'

Nana, I do not want this sort of collected purport of the whole stanza. Give Me each word, its grammatical force and meaning.

Then Nana explained it word by word.

Baba – Nana, is it enough to merely make prostration?

Nana – I do not know any other meaning for the world *pranipata* than making prostration.

Baba – What is *Pariprashenana*?

Nana – Asking questions.

Baba – What does *prashna* mean?

Nana – The same (questioning).

Baba – If *pariparashnena* means the same as *prashna* (questioning) why did Vyasa add the prefix *pari*. Was Vyasa off his head?

Nana – I do not know of any other meaning for the word *pariprashnena*.

Baba – *Seva*, what sort of *seva* is meant?

Nana – Just what we are always doing.

Baba – Is it enough to render such service?

Nana – I do not know what more is signified by that word *seva*(service).

Baba – In the next line *upadeshyanto te jananam*, can you so read it as to read anyother word in lieu of *jnanma* (birth)?

Nana – Yes.

Baba – What word?

Nana – *Ajnanam*.

Baba – Taking that word (instead) of *jnana*, is any meaning made out of the verse?

Nana – No, Shankara Bhashya gives no such construction.

Baba – Never mind if he does not. Is there any objection to using the word *ajnana* if it gives a better sense?

Nana – I do not understand how to construe by placing *ajnana* in it.

Baba – Why does Krishna refer Arjuna to *jnanis* or *tattwadarshi* to do this prostration, interrogation and service? Was not Krishna a *tattwadarshi*, in fact *jnana* itself?

Nana – Yes. He was. But I do not make out why he referred Arjuna to *jnanis*.

Baba – Have you not understood this?

Nana was humiliated. His pride was knocked on the head. Then Baba began to explain:

'It is not enough merely to prostrate before the jnanis. We must make *sarvaswa sharanagat* (complete surrender) to the Guru. Mere questioning is not enough. The question must not be asked with any improper motive to trap the Guru and catch him at mistakes in answer or out of idle curiosity. It must be serious and with a view to achieving *moksha* or spiritual progress. *Seva* is not rendering service, retaining still the feeling that one is free to offer or refuse service. One must feel that he is not the master of the body, that the body is guru's and exists merely to render service to Him. If this is done, the *Sad-guru* will show you what the *jnana* referred to in the previous stanza is.'

Baba added:

Pranipata implies surrender. Surrender must be of body, mind and wealth. Why should Krishna refer Arjuna to other *jnanis*? "*Sadhakas* take everything to be Vasudev (B. G. VII-19), i.e., any Guru takes a disciple o Vasudev and Krishna treats both as his *prana* and *atma*. As Sri Krishna knows that there are such *Bhaktas* and Gurus, he refers Arjuna to them so that their greatness may increase and be known.

A perusal of '*Shri Sai Sat Charita*' clearly bears out that Shirdi Sai Baba laid greatest emphasis on the universally acclaimed spiritual discipline of egolessness, detachment and surrender which Lord Krishna taught in the *Gita*.

Bhishma in '*Shanti Parva*' of the *Mahabharata* advised advised the Pandavas as follows:

"Truthful speech is commendable; more commendable is speech directed to do good; in my opinion that is truth which is the greatest benefit to living beings."

In Sri Shirdi Sai Baba's teachings this very concept of truthful conduct directed towards the good of others finds a place of pride. How poignant and forcefully penetrating are His following words:

"You must always adhere to truth and fulfill all the promises you make. Have *Shraddha* (faith) and *saburi* (patience) then I will always be with you wherever you are."

". . . Restrain yourself from forbidden food and drinks. Avoid needless disputation. Avoid falsehood. Have restraint of speech."

". . . You have got to make *vichar* or make enquiry about your true nature."

Universality, humanism and tolerance have been the most essential traits of *Sanatana Dharma*. '*Sathyam, Shivam, Sundram*' are the three highest universal values of Hinduism. The eternal question "*Who am I?*", which engaged the attention of almost all the Vedic sages and that of Ramana Maharishi, a contemporary of Shirdi Sai Baba, was also often posed by Baba to His devotees. He advised them to ponder over "Who am I?"

The great saint of Soth Indis Ramana Maharishi advised:

"When other thoughts arise, one should not pursue then, but should inquire, but should inquire: To whom did they arise? It does not matter how many thoughts arise. As each though arises, one should inquire with diligence, "To whom has this thought arisen?" The answer that would emerge be, "To me". Thereupon if one inquires, "Who am I?", the mind will go back to its source; and the thought that arose will become quiescent. With repeated practice in this manner, the mind will develop the skill to stay in its source... Whatever one does, one should not do with the egoity "I". If once acts in that way, all will appear as of the nature of Shiva (God)."

'*Shri Sai Sat Charita*' records as incident of a Marwadi (businessman) who had come to Shirdi Sai Baba with prayer to show him *Brahma gyan* or self-realization. Baba's instructions to him were:

"For seeing *Brahma gyan* one has to give five things, i.e., surrender five things: (1) Five *Pranas* (vital forces); (2) Five *Indriyas* (senses); (3) *Mana* (mind); (4) *Buddhi* (intellect); and *Aham* (ego).

"...How can he whose mind is engrossed in wealth, progeny and prosperity, expect to know the *Brahma* without removing his attachment for the same?"

Shirdi Sai Baba did not extol the virtue of one's taking *sanyas*. He advised His devotees to lead normal family lives, to live in society and yet remain detached, pure and elevated. The concept of *moksha* (liberation) is one of the most important concepts of Hinduism. For that end, several modes of worship, penance, fasts, rituals and other prescription like *japa*, *tapa* and the like have been prescribed. Shirdi Sai Baba did not want His devotees to be confused and get lost in the rigmarole of liberation but just to do these four things – to have *Shraddha* (faith) and *saburi* (patience); to do *namasmaran* (name chanting), to surrender to Guru, and to do duties of one's station in life honestly and properly in a detached manner.

In Islam, the values of respect for the rights of the fellow beings, equality, mercy, justice, characterfulness, piety, tolerance, peace, forgiveness, hospitality, perseverance, courage etc., have been emphasized. Islam presents a very clear concept of God:

"There is no God save Him, the living, the eternal. Neither slumber nor sleep overtakes Him. Unto Him belongeth whatever is in the Heavens and whatever is in the earth. Who can intercede with Him save by His own leave? He knoweth that which is in front of them and that which is behind them. He is the Sublime, the Magnificent."

Let us see these teachings of Shirdi Sai Baba and we shall immediately know that they are quite identical with the Islamic values and the Islamic conception of God mentioned above:

"Sitting in this *Masjid* I shall never, never speak untruth. Take pity on Me like this. First give bread to the hungry, then eat yourself. Not this well. *Sri Hari* (God) will certainly be pleased if you give water to the thirsty, bread to the hungry, clothes to the naked and your verandah to strangers for sitting and resting. . . Let anybody speak hundreds of things against you, do not resent by giving any bitter reply. If you always tolerate such things, you will certainly be happy. Let the world go topsy-turvy, you remain where you are. Standing or staying in your own place, look on calmly at the show of all things passing before you. . . Demolish wall of difference that separates you and Me."

".*Allah Malik hai*", i.e., "*Allah* is the Sole Proprietor, nobody else is our Protector. His method of work is extraordinary, invaluable, and inscrutable. His will be done and He will show us the way and satisfy our heart's desires. God is, consider it as truth, God is not, consider this as untruth, Everything is *Allah*'s, only *Allah*. All this is Allah Mian's.

God is the Master, none else it. His actions are extraordinary and inscrutable. None is greater than *Allah* who gave you birth, who looked after you.

Reading these words of Baba, one feels as if Prophet Mohammed Himself were speaking through the mouth of Shirdi Sai Baba. He believed in one God and *"Allah Malik"* was His constant refrain.

Jesus Christ's two commandments 'Love of God' and love of Neighbours' and the universally acclaimed emphasis on prayer, worship and service are the greatest contributions of Christianity to humanity. This very universal value of Love found its highest culmination in the life and teachings of Shirdi Sai Baba as the Universal Master, the kind of which the world had not yet known. He not only preached but by His daily behavior and life activities exemplified the genuine love nad concern He had not only for men, women and children, but even for animals, birds and insects. Countless religious and spiritual personalities and scriptures throughout the 8,000 years old cultural history of mankind have been repeating the importance of love as a supreme human value which cements hearts and elevates man to divinity, but none had ever given such a direct, empirical and thrilling demonstration of love in action as was done by Shirdi Sai Baba who in numerous incidents of His stunning miracles like appearing in the forms of a hungry dog, a pig, a buffalo, a beggar, a *sadhu*, an ant, insects or the like, accepted food offered by His devotees, or took over the illness, grievous wounds and scorching heat of the blacksmith's fireplace inflicted on innocent human beings and animals.

In a simple yet grand and thrilling manner, He demonstrated each time that all creatures have the same *atma* and therefore all must be loved by us as we love ourselves. As Christ used to say, "All are one, be like everyone." Shirdi Sai Baba shared His food with His devotees, dogs, cats, birds, insects freely, and loved them all equally without the least trace of differentiation. Nowhere, not even in the stories of *Puranas* which are full of all sorts of thrilling stories of miracles, do we come across such thrilling demonstrations of genuine love which Shirdi Sai Baba showed for the world. Indeed, there have been innumerable miracle men in the long history of mankind but Shirdi Sai Baba was the first one in the world to use His miracle making powers to teaching illiterate and semi-illiterate people who could not understand the intricate scriptures, the two basic principles of spirituality – the principle of *atma* common to all creatures and the principle of love. Thus Sri Shirdi Sai Baba's stature as the Universal Master legitimately and mainly rests on this sort of unprecedented exemplification of empirical evidence of the universal element or power of love on which the whole cosmos is held together and functions.

Sikhism like Islam, upholds the concept of One God, and the same was preached by Shirdi Sai Baba all His life through word and deed. Also *Guru Nanak's* most remarkable elucidation of Guru's importance in the life of a disciple finds its total replication in the memoirs and the teachings of Shirdi Sai Baba. The common refrain of both was that one cannot gain anything without achieving Guru's grace. Guru Nanak sang:

Without the Guru, one goes astray and transmigrates,
Without the Guru, the efforts become useless,
Without the Guru, the man serves furiously,

Without the Guru, one is not satisfied in *maya*,

Without the Guru, one loses at every step, says Nanak.

Comparing this with what Shirdi Sai Baba said about Guru to

His devotee Mrs. Radhabai Deshmukh said:

"Oh mother, my *Guru* never taught me any *mantra*; then how shall I blow any *mantra* in your ears? Just remember that Guru's tortoise-like loving glance gives us happiness. Do not try to get *mantra* or *updesh* from anybody. Make Me the sole object of your thoughts and you will, no doubt, attain *paramartha* (the spiritual goal of life)...No *sadhana*, nor proficiency in the six *shsastrs*, are necessary. Have faith and confidence in your Guru. Believe fully that Guru is the sole actor or doer. Blessed is he who knows the greatness of his Guru and thinks him to be *Hari, Hara* and *Brahma* (*Trimurti* incarnate)."

To his another devotee Pant, Baba instructed thus:

"Come what may, leave not but stick to your bolster (support i.e. Guru) and ever remain steady, always be in union with him."

Professor G.G. Narke confessed said:

"According to Sai Baba traditions, the disciple or devotee who comes to the feet of the Guru in complete surrender has to be no doubt pure, chaste and virtuous... The Guru does not teach. He radiates influence. That influence is poured in and absorbed with full benefit by the soul which has completely surrendered itself, blotting out the self....The Guru will lift him, endow him with higher powers, vaster knowledge and increasing realization of truth. And the end is safe in the Guru's hands. All this was not uttered by Sai Baba at one breath to me or within my hearing, but the various hints I got from his example and dealings with many and His occasional words — when put together, amount to this."

Ram Chandra Sita Ram Dev alias Bala bhau or Bal bhat of Andheri, who had first seen Shirdi Sai Baba in 1908, asked Baba to give him *updesh* and be his *Guru*.To him Baba said:

"It is not essential that one should have a *Guru*. Everything is within us. What you sow, so you reap. What you give, you get. There is no need for a Guru. It is all within you. Try to listen within and follow the direction you get. We must look at ourself. That is the monitor, the *Guru*."

Although during the last decade of His life (1908-18), He was literally rolling in wealth as He was getting *dakshina* of about 500 to 1,000 rupees per day, yet He invariably distributed the whole of it among His devotees and beggars and poor people retaining almost nothing with Him. At the time of His *Maha Samadhi*, only an amount of Rs. 16 in cash was found in His belongings as testified by Chakra Narayan who was Police fouzdar at Koparagon and present there at Shirdi in October 1918 when Baba passed away:

Whatever *dikshina*(donations) He got daily He was paying or giving away hundreds of rupee When He died, we took possession of His cash; that was only Rs.16.

In the film *Shirdi Ke Sai Baba* there is a scene in which a *sadhu* comes from Haridwar to Shirdi and is amazed to see the grandeur of Shirdi Sai Baba's *palki* procession from Dwarka Mai to *chavadi*, and wonders how a saintly person like Sai Baba prefers all this pomp and show; he takes Baba to be a hypocrite. But when he comes near Baba in <u>Dwaraka Mai Masjid</u> and questions Baba about it, Baba shows him His miracle – giving the glimpse of the sadhu's Guru, which immediately brings him to the feet of Sai Baba.

In Sai literature, we find such references that in later years Baba used to receive plates full of delicious foods from His devotees, girls used to come and dance before Him in the *Masjid*, people used to decorate Him with costly *chadars* (shawls) and clothes, He held His durbar like a majestic ruler. Yet, He was utterly indifferent to all this paraphernalia and accepted all this as an imposition of the wishes of His devotees of Him.

The following testimonies of Baba's contemporary devotees are most relevant in this respect:

Mrs. Manager testified as under:

"He (Baba) had no interests to serve or protect, no institution to seek support for or maintain: no acquisitions to safeguard; no private property to feel anxious about. Everything He got was quickly disposed of. He lived on the begged and freely offered food...When He died, He left in His pocket just the amount needed for His funeral expenses. His self-control and equanimity may be mentioned in this connection. He was far too lofty to care for trivial things. His palate, like His other senses, was so strictly things. His palate, like His other senses, was so strictly under His control that none ever found Him to show any desire for anything, so far as I know."

Das Ganu recalled:

"Several of those that he was regularly paying everyday were subjected to income tax. After Lokmanya Tilak visited Baba (1915-1917), the Income tax department directed its attention to the Shirdi *Samsthan*, some officer came and watched the income. They first wanted to tax Sai Baba, but (perhaps seeing that He had little left with Him to proceed upon) they taxed His regular donors, viz, Tatya Patel, Bade Baba, Bagla and Bayaji Patel.

... He was really *advaita* personified. Thirty-two dancing girls would come and play before Him daily; He would never care to look at them. He never cared for anything. He was detached and in His *anand* state...

He used to cure the money–mindedness and the ego of His devotees by asking for *dakshina* repeatedly till they were left with no money. He advised none to become a *sanyasi* and forsake his family and home. He advised His devotees like Nana Saheb and Khaparde not to lust for sex. He advised Mlahaspati to sleep very little at night when he used to sleep with Baba in the *Dwarka Mai Masjid*."

In short, He Himself was following the kind of *yoga* which Guru Nanak spoke about while replying to siddha Lohadipa Yogi, and He advised His spiritually advanced devotees to follow the same scrupulously.

Where else except in the divine personality and role-functioning style of Shirdi Sai Baba do we find located in one personality the vibrant elements of Lord Krishna's superb magnetism of love and knowledge of the reality of *atmagyan*, Buddha's aura of compassion sand piety, Adi Shankara's *advaitism* and spirited fight against castes and sects and strict orthodox, Kabir's unconventional scathing attack on bigotry and obscurantism, Tulsi's devotion to Lord Rama and the devotional outpourings of love for the divine as those of the great integration like Mira, Chaitanya, Nanak, Purandharadasa, Thyagaraja, Kanakadas, Tukaram, Ramadas, Narasimham, Mehta Ramanand, Nayanar Apar, Eknath, Namdev, Manikkavachakak, etc.; the mysticism of Rama Krishna Paramhansa and the love, brotherhood and service taught by Christ, Mohammed, Mother Teresa, Dalai Lama, Baba Amte and the like, and the philosophical musings of Ramana Maharshi, Sri Aurobindo and others? Sri Shirdi Sai Baba epitomized the quintessence of the values and ideals taught by the world's greatest religious and spiritual masters of all religions and lands in history.

People of all religions, nations and cultures have been and will always be finding all the previous values and spiritual truths in the life of Shirdi Sai Baba. Therefore, it is fully justified calling Shirdi Sai Baba the Universal Master of mankind – a unique *avatar* of God who descended in order to promote sublime form of spirituality and emotional integration among all human beings. The like of Him, who combined in His personality so diverse and ennobling attributes and lived such a simple life of *faqir*, has not yet seen by the world, and who knows, the like of Him may not again be born at all! This makes Him a unique Universal Master of mankind whose most inspiring and spiritually elevating life story should be made known to people of all races, religions and lands.

One thing which is all the more unique about this great Universal Master is that although He shed His mortal coils in 1918, yet He even today He responds to the earnest yearnings and prayers of all people in distress and of all His devotees as per unique assurances given by Him. We do not know of any other spiritual personality who had ever made such grand and compassionate assurances to mankind which still keep getting fulfilled. Evidently, a lot of research into the divine mysteries of Shirdi Sai Baba as the unique Universal Master of mankind is needed in order to understand Him. Baba's own advice in this connection was:

"If a man utters My name with love, I shall fulfill all his wishes, increase his devotion. If he earnestly listens to My life and deeds, him I shall be set in front and back and on all sides."

His holiness Dalai Lama, the spiritual Head of the Tibetans, while delivering the Ninth Bhimsen Sachar Memorial lecture on 'Spiritual Values in Modern India', organized by the Servants of the People Society at Lajpat Bhawan, New Delhi, on 3 December, 1980, said:

The qualities of love and compassion are universals qualities which various religions try to develop among their adherents but religion is not a prerequisite which may be said to constitute a universal religion in them. You don't need a complicated philosophy; you don't need a temple to develop these qualities.

Shirdi Sai Baba's total emphasis and compassion as has been shown above, was on such universal values like love, which are the basics of spirituality. He was not a promoter or champion of any religion as such; instead He was the teacher of spirituality which does not need a complicated philosophy. That is why, Shirdi Sai Baba did not advance any complicated philosophy of His own, but emphasized the universal values and qualities.

The religions may, in future, change or even disappear, as Acharya Rajneesh once sai, but the super spirituality of such simple universal values as preached and practiced by Shirdi Sai Baba will ever remain alive and growing.

Chapter – 7
Sri Shirdi Sai Baba's Popularity

Since Sri Shirdi Sai Baba attained *Maha Samadhi* in 1918, His name and fame as a very great and highly benevolent and merciful saint, God's incarnation of a very high stature, have been spreading throughout the world. In a miraculous manner, thousands of people of different religions and nationalities are becoming His devotees each day having come under the fold of His magnanimous grace and experiencing some sort of thrilling miracle in their lives. Temples devoted to Him have been coming up in different places, cities, towns and villages in India as well as in far off lands Like USA, UK, Australia and African countries, Singapore, etc., due to the efforts of highly devoted self-motivated people. Innumerable devotees and rich donors vie with each other in providing funds and material for building and furnishing Shirdi Sai temples that are coming up throughout the world as inspired by Him in many invisible and mysterious ways. Many charitable hospitals are run besides these temples and many welfare services and other charitable activities are being carried out by enthusiastic people in the name of Sri Shirdi Sai Baba. The number of devotees visiting Shirdi is ever increasing. In a nutshell, the devotional cult of Sri Shirdi Sai Baba is fast spreading throughout the world.

It is only because of Baba's mysterious divine wish and design that all these unique things are happening and Baba's eminence is fast spreading in concentric circles in all lands and all communities. Why is it that the appeal of Shirdi Sai Baba's charismatic personality is so irresistible to people?

Sai devotee, B. Ramanatha Rao of Sai Kutir, Madras, has advanced the following reasons for it:

1. First and foremost because, in the words of Hemadpant, the author of *Shri Sai Sat Charita*, He (Shirdi Sai Baba) had taken a vow to give you what you want.

2. And that too immediately cash down; you ask with sincere devotion *(Shraddha)* and patience *(saburi)* and there is the result.

3. He is so easily pleased. No hard penance, no unbearable fasts, not even difficult concentration and control of senses. In His words, "You look to Me and I will look to you." Can there be anything simpler than this?

4. He left His mortal body years ago and even today thousands of devotees have experienced His presence, having met their demands. What more guarantee is required?

5. Not being bodily present as a human being today, there is no danger of being cheated in His worship. In the case of so many *avatars, Bhagawans,* and *yogis* who have cropped up at present in the country, one is not sure if one is following the real preceptor *(Sadguru)*.

6. No money is required to worship Baba. He is pleased even with flowers, fruits, leaves or even water, devotionally offered. You do not even have to spend for travelling up to Shirdi. He is available even where you are, "even beyond the seven seas".

7. Ashes *(udi)* from the fire burning eternally in His *Dwarka Mai* is the cheapest and most infallible medicine for all diseases. The cost is only two-paise – faith and patience.

8. His life history written by Hemadpant contains all the wisdom of the *Vedas,* the *Upanishsads* and the *Gita* in the form of simple stories and anecdotes. Reading them alone and following the advice, therein, one can reach the goal of liberation without fail.

9. Repetition of His name *'Sat'* is so short, so sweet and so easy to pronounce; no twisting of tongue and difficult accents.

10. Last but not least, He on fulfilling your demands in this world, ensures that you do not get caught up in the dangerous web of this *sansar*, so He slowly moulds you, guides you and takes you step by step to liberation which is the key to eternal and everlasting bliss.

Shirdi Sai Baba's main insistence was on morality and simple and essential laws of spirituality which are universally emphasized by all religious scriptures, moral leaders and great personalities of all races and nations not on ritualistic religion as such. In matters of religion, He preached integration or unity of the genuine kind. He emphasized that all human beings and creatures have the same *atma* and, therefore, all are one and everyone in the living world is entitled to receive our love, care, hospitality, concern and help.

The world, as it is, is full of so many dissensions and social, cultural, economic and political conflicts, jealousies and immoral, disjunctive and dysfunctional tendencies which have made the life of human beings all over the world very insecure. Religions have disappointed humanity through the doings of many fundamentalist, fanatics, hypocrites and wealth loving and power-hankering Godmen, *yogis* and *acharayas* who rarely see eye to eye among themselves and do not feel shy in openly condemning each other.

In such a social and religious context of the contemporary world, Shirdi Sai Baba alone comes up to the expectations of the masses of the world as the ideal Godman who epitomizes simplicity, spirituality, love and genuine concern for all creatures, of the highest order. He combined in Him all the finest traits of the Vedic gods, Adi Shankara, Christ, Buddha, Mahavir, Zoroaster, Mohammed, Nanak and all other great spiritual and religious personalities born in the world. Shirdi Sai Baba's charisma based on His simplicity, unconventionality lack of diehard ritualism, love and stress on unity and harmony is in utter contrast of the affluent and controversial lifestyles of many of the contemporary Godmen, *yogis* and *acharyas* captivates the hearts of people and is more than thereof anyone of the modern saints and Godmen. He is the most ideal saint who comes up to the expectations of most people of the world. The world is fed up with all those who teach religion, morality, spirituality and yoga and the like in enchanting words but crave for worldly properties, publicity, political patronage and all the pleasures and luxuries of modern life. Sri Shirdi Sai Baba, therefore, impresses us most.

It is also true that generally the modern educated people do not have much fascination for die-hard ritualism. They do not have patience to do any kind of elaborate penance, *yagna*, *dhyana* or the like. They crave for simple, easy, ready-made, instant benefits even in spiritual matters. They are cosmopolitan, secular and universal in their outlook and, therefore, do not wish to be confined to the narrow walls of their traditional religion and complicated incomprehensible rituals and customs. They crave for a broader, more sublime and easier-to-understand kind of spiritual experience. Shirdi Sai Baba's simple teachings are without any trappings of a complicated philosophy and His grace can be available to them just on remembering Him without any kind of difficulty or special effort.

Sri Shirdi Sai Baba had givn eleven assurances of protection and wishfulfillment to all the visitorshic contemporary as well future ones.They have proved true my all and believers le throughout have faith in then and so they have been coming in hordes verydy.On an average about 20,000 people visit Shirdi dail and on Thursday and every Hindu festival the number of visitors invariably swells upto 100000 and even more. Even some foreigners come here toreceive sai Baba's egansary grace,

It is because of these solid reasons that Shirdi Sai Baba's name and fame have been spreading so fast throughout the world during the preceding eight decades and it continues to spread with ever growing tempo.

How Baba's name is spreading

Sri Shirdi Sai *Sansthan* (Trust), Shirdi, has been publishing valuable books and pictorial albums on Baba which have been spreading Baba's name and message throughout the world. Besides this, a number of organizations and voluntary bodies have come up to spread Baba's message. Sri Narasimha Swamiji established the All India *Sai Samaj* at Madras (now called Chennai) and authored a number of valuable books on Bbaa and spread His name and message throughout India. Sri Sai Sharananadji, Baba's noted contemporary devotee, authored a book '*Shri Sai Bab,* in Marathi and, *Sri Sai The Superman.* which have made Baba known throughout the world. Swami Karunananda had his son Shri Narayana Swami of Bhagawati Sai Sansthan, Panwel (Maharashtra) have been instrumental in spreading the teachings of Baba through their books, lectures and pioneering efforts to establish Sri Shirdi Sai Temples in U K, USA, Africa, Australia, etc. Sri Sai Samaj, Picket, Secundrabad (Andhra Pradesh), Sai Bhakta Samaj, Delhi (Shirdi Sai Temple, 17, Institutional Area, Lodhi Road, New Delhi), Shirdi Sai Sabha, Chandigarh and other organizations have for years been doing remarkable service in the propagation of the message of Shirdi Sai Baba.

In Karnataka, a number of Shirdi Sai Temples have been established by the individual efforts of a highly devoted soul, Sri H.D. Laxman Swami, Sri Shivamma Thayee of Bangalore, a contemporary devotee of Shirdi Sai Baba inaugurated a number of Sri Shirdi Sai Temples and herself established three statues of Baba on His directions in her Sri Shirdi Sai Ashram, Roopen Agrahara, Maliwala, Bangalore.

In Rajasthan, a old devotee, Kailash Bakiwala, has estabglished a Shirdi Sai Temple at village Kukas, 17 Kms from Jaipur on the Jaipur-Delhi road.

It has been the experience of not only Kailash Bakiwala, H.D. Laxman Swamiji and Shivamma Thayee but of almost all those who have been establishing Shirdi Sai Temples that Baba Himself has, through His mysterious ways, unknown persons and in strange circumstances, been ensuring that the construction and furnishing activities of the temples being newly constructed are carried out unexpectedly by the timely help in cash as well as kind at every step. Someone strangely to donate land, someone to donate the required bags of cement, someone comes up with the offer to provide fans, windows, etc., someone with funds to purchase marbles and so on, without anyone asking for these things. These mysterious divine happenings are heard wherever one tries to discover how the new Sai Temples are coming up throughout.

At many places, still more thrilling things (these are certainly miracles) have happened which have led to the establishment of Sri Shirdi Sai temples on certain spots. Thus, for instance, several years back at Coimbatore a big cobra appeared and stayed there at a *bhajan* session for several hours. People were convinced that it was nothing else but Sri Shirdi Sai Baba Himself and then a huge Nag Sai Temple was built on that very spot which has been attracting thousands of visitors every year. On the Internet anyone find details of this great snake miracle, the temple and Sri Nag Sai Trust in Coimbatore. Thistemple wa sinaugurared bt Sri Sathya Sai Baba.. I had also visited it in Coimbatore many years back, A brief write up on this miracle available on the intrrenet is as under:

'In 1943 on the evening of the 7th of January, *Guru-vara* (Thursday) sacred for worship of Baba, a miracle happened! A shining and lustrous nsga (Cobra) small in size but possessing an unusually big hoad with divine marks of *Tripundra, Shankh*a and Chakra appeared before Baba's picture when the *Bhajan* was going on in full swing to the accompaniment of drum cymbals etc., with all the lights on. The *Naga* (cobra) stood there in a pose of worship fullness entranced in Baba music! Waving of lights, *aratis* etc had no effect on the nerves of the Cobra. People around who had swelled into a crowd of a few hundred stood there in awe and wonder at the wondrous sight of the *Naga* with spread head. There was no fear for the snake; the proverb that even a battalion of soldiers of valour shiver at the sight of a cobra was falsified- young and old, women and children in thousands began to pour into the spacious land of the

Bhajan maidan to witness the *Naga* that lingered in the same spot for full 48 hours, Baba *bhaktas* (devotees) began to shower baskets after baskets of flowers in worshipful reverence for the *Naga*. The Cobra was virtually submerged in a mound of flowers but even then, he was unmobile .Arti was performed for **the Naga.**

On the second day of *Naga's* advent,a photographer came to take a picture of the Naga in its majesty but the latter was immersed under heaps of flowers. No one had the courage of go near the spot where the cobra ws lodged and clear the flowers. The only course open to them was to pray ho! the Naga jumped out of the flowers heaps and posed for the photograph as if in answer to the prayers of the multitude. One and all were sure for the first time that it was all the work of Sai Baba. The devotees then prayed with fervour and faith to the *Naga* to clear out and enable them to resort to their routine worship of Baba in the *maidan.* Then the immobile Naga showed signs of movements, it went around Sri Sai Baba's picture and slowly marched out into the open and disappeared into bush where later an ani-hill (snake's natural habitat) appeared. The place where the Naga disappeared in held as a 'Holy Ground' by devotees and from that day onwards Shirdi Sai Baba in Coimbatore is worshipped as "*Sri Nagasai*".

Miracles have indeed happened and every day happening with countless people at many places in India and broad. Many Sri Shirdi Sai Temples have sprung up throughout India and in many foreighn countries. Guru ji C.b. Sarpathy has motoivated the establisdment of over 200 ShirdiSai templses.. The name and fame of Baba and His universal message have thus been spreading all over. Instances like these compel even the extreme rationalists and iconoclasts among the modernites to believe in the mysterious supernatural powers and divine will of Shirdi Sai Baba which makes such things possible in the materialistic and selfish world of today.

There are many self-inspired and self-motivated devotees of Sri Shirdi Sai Baba belonging to Hindu, Jain, Christian, Zoproastrian, Sikh and major and tribal religions who on their own havenbeen writing and publishing books on Baba, doing social welfare activities for the poor and organizing Sai *kirtans* and *bhajan* sessions for moral and spiritual uplift of mankind. Considerations of religion, race, caste, nationality, class, etc., do not come in the way of anyone becoming a Sai devotee and propagator of Baba's message. Thus, for instance, Zarine Taraporewalla, the English translator of Das Ganu's famous

Stavan Manjari and K.J. Bhishma's *Sainath Sagunopasana* is a Parsee Lady; Kailash Bakiwala of Jaipur, the founder of Sri Shirdi Sai Temple at Kukas (near Achrol, Jaipur district, Rajasthan) is a Jain; Bashir Baba, a great follower and propagator of Sri Shirdi Sai Baba (some believe that He Himself was Baba's incarnation) was a Muslim. There are many other such examples of devotees belonging to other religions who are great devotees of Baba. There are also some foreign Christians of Austria, Australia and Canada who are great devotees of Shirdi Sai Baba. At Shirdi, one could during 1990s see a middle-aged African lady attired in a white robe like a nun moving about *Gurusthan*, *Chavadi* and *Dwarka Mai* constantly or sitting with Sri Shivnesh Swamiji at *Gurusthan* and singing Kabir's songs at the *bhajan* sessions at *Chavadi*.

All these concrete examples testify to the fact that the universal nature of Shirdi Sai Baba and the greatness and uniqueness of his divine message of brotherhood and love have indeed been understood by many enlightened people of different racial, religious and national backgrounds. Baba's Spiritual Socialism has won the hearts of many people and the impact of His magnetism is thus going to attract more and more people's souls towards Him.

Prominent Shirdi Sai Temples & Centrrs in the World

Sri Shirdi Sai Baba's name and fame has spread all over the world. There are countless Shirdi Sai Baba temples and centres in India and in a number of foreign countries. Given below are the prominent ones among as far as known to me:

- Shirdi Sai Baba Temple, Shirdi (Maharashtra)
- Shirdi Sai Baba Temple, Coimbatore (Tamil Nadu)
- Shirdi Sai Baba Temple, Bharat Nagar, Chennai
- Shirdi Sai Baba Temple, Kolhapur (Maharashtra)
- Shidi Sai Baba Temple, Sholapur (Maharashtra)
- Shirid Sai Baba Temple, Khar (West) Mumbai (Maharashtra)
- Shirid Sai Baba Temple, Mylapore, Chennai
- Shirid Sai Baba Temple, Bharat Nagar, Chennai
- Shirid Sai Baba Temple, Lodhi Road, New Delhi
- Shirid Sai Baba Temple, Shirdi (Maharashtra)
- Shirid Sai Baba Temple, Sector 16A, Faridabad

- Shirid Sai Baba Temple, Chandigarh
- Shirid Sai Baba Temple, Sector 25, NOIDA (U.P.)
- Shirid Sai Baba Temple, Sector 40, NOIDA
- Shirid Sai Baba Temple, Gurgaon (Haryana)
- Shirid Sai Baba Temple, Agra, Chippitola, Agra (U.P.)
- Shirid Sai Baba Temple, Aligarh (U.P.)
- Shirid Sai Baba Temple, Shirdi (Maharashtra)
- Shirid Sai Baba Temple, Jaipur (Rajasthan)
- Shirid Sai Baba Temple, Kukas, Jaipur (Rajasthan)
- Shirid Sai Baba Temple, Bank Colony, Hyderabad
- Shirdi Sai Baba Temple, Moradabad (U.P.)
- Shirdi Sai Baba Temple, Bareilly (U.P.)
- Shirdi Sai Baba Temple, Sapnawat (U.P.)
- Shirdi Sai Baba Temple, Shirdi Sai Temple, Shastri Nagar, Meerut
- Shirdi Sai Baba Temple, Illford, (U.K.)
- Shirdi Sai Baba Centre, Forida, Inverness (U.S.A.)
- Shirdi Sai Baba Temple, 45-16, Robinson Street, Flushing, New York
- Shirdi Sai Baba Temple, Bronswick, New Jersey (U.S.A.)
- Shirdi Sai Baba Ambers Creek, Flushing, Pittsberg (U.S.A.)
- Shirdi Sai Baba Temple, Chicagoland, Hampshire (U.S.A.)
- Shirdi Sai Baba Temple, Hurlington House, Nathan Road, Tsim Tsa Tsui,

Kowloon, Hongkong

There are many Shirdi Sai Baba Temples in Himachal Pradesh, U.P., Andhra Pradesh, Tamil Nadu, Odessa and other states in India and in foreign countries like Mauritius but we do not know their exact addresses yet. Many of these(about 200) temples have been started by the efforts of Guruji C.B.Satpathi, who is a highly inspired *pracharak* of Sri Shirdi Sai Baba.

Important Shirdi Sai Baba Organizations

- All India Sai Samaj Mylapore, Chennai. (T.N.)
  Sai Publications, Red Cross Road, Civil Lines, Nagpur (Maharashtra)
- Dwarakamayi Publications, Hyderabad-500033 (A.P.)

- Shri Bhagwati Sai Sansthan, Panvel-410206 (Maharashtra) (Sai Sevak Narayan Baba, Spiritual Head).
- Sai Foundation India, New Delhi-110060: H-353, New Rajinder Nagar.
- Sai Prachar Kendra, S.C.F. 18, Sector 19-D, Chandigarh-160 019.
- Sri Sai Spiritual Centre, T. Nagar, Bangalore-560 028.
- Sri Sai Samaj, Picket, Secunderabad (A.P.)
- Sri Sai Baba *Sansthan*, Shirdi (Maharashtra)
- Sri Sai Samaj Calcutta, P-113, Lake Terrace, Calcutta-700 029
- Sai Sudha Trust, Shirdi Sai Bab Mandir, Garkhal, Kausauli (H.P.)-173 201
- Sri Bhakta Parivar, 91, Napier Town, Jabalpur (M.P.)
- International Pragya Mission, Saket, New Delhi-110017. (Swami Pragyanand, Founder President).
- Akhil Bhartiya Shirdi Sai Bhakti Mahasabha, Hyderabad. (M. Rangacharya President).
- Akhanda Sainama Saptaha Samithi, B/3/F-15, Krupa Complex, Ananda Bagh, Hyderabad- 500 047. (A.P.) (D. Shankariah, Secretary).
- Shirdi Sai Baba Web Site Organization 182, West Melrose Street, Suite No. 4,South Elgin,
  1L 60177, U.S.A.
  Phone: 847-931-4058
  Fax: 847-931-4066
  Web: http://www.saibaba.org
  E-mail: maildrop@saibaba.org
  (Mukund Raj, Web Site Administrator)

- Shirdi Sai Temple
  46-16 Robinson Street, Flushing,
  New York (U.S.A.)
  Tel: (718) 3219243

- Shirdi Sai Baba Sansthan of America,
  625, Summerset Country,
  Richwater Township, New Jersey-08807 (U.S.A.)
  Tel.: (908) 3061420

- Shirdi Sai Foundation Centre,
  4901, Pleasant Grove, Inverness,
  Florida – 34452 (U.S.A.)
  Tel.: (352) – 8602181

- Sai Foundation, Kenya (Africa)
  P.O. Box 41409, Nairobi, Kenya
  E-mail: ushmid@africaonline.com

- Shri Shatha Shruga Vidhya Samasthe [®]
  Magadi Main Road,
  Bangalore – 560079, (Phone: 3486044)

- Shirdi Sai Baba Satsang,
  KBRS Bldg., Near Velu Mudaliar Dispensary,
  Kamaraj Road, Bangalore – 560042
  Phone Off.: 5300225, Res.: 5300116

- Shri Saibaba Sansthan Trust
  P.O.: Shirdi tal. Rahata Dist. Ahmednagar, Maharashtra State, India
  Phone: +91-2423-258500 (30 lines)
  Fax No.: +91-2423-258870, P.R.O. Office: +91-2423-258770
  E-mail: saibaba@sai.org.in
  URL: http://www.shrisaibabasansthan.org/ & http://www.sai.org.in

- "International Sri Sai Consciousness Foundation Centre"
  Venue: "Sri Sai Sharanalaya" Premises
  II Main, Nagarabhavi Main Road
  Sanjeevini Nagar, Moodalapalya
  Bangalore – 560 072

- Shirdi Sai Baba Old Age Home Educational Trust
  Plot No. 124, 4th Main Road, Sundara Babu Nagar,
  Veppampattur, Thiruvallur Dist.
  Ph.: 044-27620950, Cell: 9840081877

- All India Akhanda Sai Nama Seva Samithi
  A.K.S. Shruthi, Flat No. S-18, Second Floor, 63, K.K. Road, Venkatapuram,
  Ambattur, Chennai-600 053, Tel.: 044-2657-3496
  R. Radhakrishna (Sai Jeevi) Chief Patron

Journals Devoted to Sri Shirdi Sai Baba

1. *Sai Chetna* (English), Chennai, Sri Sai Baba Spiritual & Charitable Trust, Injambakkam, Chennai-600 041.
2. *Sai Kripa* (English & Hindi). New Delhi-110003) Shri Sai Bhakta Samaj, 17, Institutional Area, Lodhi Road, New Delhi.
3. *Sai Kripa*: (Hindi) New Delhi: Sai Kripa Sansthan, A-16, Naraina II New Delhi-110 028, (Editor: Dipli Tuli).
4. *Sai Padananda*, Bangalore-560 028: Sri Sai Spiritual Centre, T. Nagar, (Editor: R. Seshadri).
5. *Sai Prabha* (English & Telugu). Hyderabad-500 027: H. No. 3-5-697/A, Telugu Academi Lane, Vittalwadi, Narayanguda.
6. *Sai Sudha*, All India Sai Samaj, Mylapore, Chennai (T.N.).
7. *Sai Sugam* (English & Tamil), Sri Shirdi Bhairava Sai Bbaa Temple Trust, 6 Bharath Nagar, Neel Kattabi Road, Madipakkarm, Chennai-600091.
8. *Shri Sai Leela* (English & Hindi), Bombay-400 014: 'Sai Niketan', 804-B, Dr. Ambedkar Road, Dadar.
9. *Sri Sai Avatars*, (English & Bengali). Calcutta-700 029: Sri Sai Samaj, Calcutta, P-113, Lake Terrace, (Editor: S.M. Bannerjee).
10. *Sri Sai Divya Sandesh*, (English & Hindi). (Distt. Raigarh): Sri Bhagawati Sai Sansthan Plot No. 400/I, Near Railway Station. Panvel-410 206.
11. *Sri Sai Spandan*, Hyderabad-500 872: Self-Analysis Institute, 402 Raj Apartments, B.H. Society, Kulkatpally (A.P.)
12. *Shradha suburi* (English & Hindi). 702, 7th Floor, Plot No. 9, Yash Apartment, Sector 11, Dwarka, New Delhi (Editor: Ruby Sharma)

Sri Shirdi Sai Baba Websites

- Annababa.com
- Baba's Eleven Promises
- From Shirdi Sai to Sathya Sai
  By Sharada Dev
- Life History of Shirdi Sai Baba
  By Sri Ammula Sambasiva Rao – Online book
- My Meeting with Baba of Shirdi
  By Shivamma Thayee
- O Sai Baba
- Reincarnation of Shirdi Sai Baba
- *Sab-ka-malik-ek*
- *Sai Aarati* and *Bhajans*
- Sai Baba of Shirdi
- Sai Baba Temple, Shirdi
- Sai Bharadwaja
- www.Saidrbarusa.org
- Shri Sai Baba Sansthan, Shirdi
- Shree Shirdi Sai Sansthan Sydney, Australia (The first Temple in Australia dedicated to Shirdi Sai Baba)
- Shri Saibaba Sansthan, Shirdi
- Shirdi Sai and Sathya Sai are One and the same
- By Arjan D. Bharwani
- Shirdi Sai Baba.com
- Shirdi Sai Baba Website
- Shirdi Sai Baba Site
- Shirdi Sai Baba on the World Wide Web
- Sai Bab Guru Srinath
- Shirdi Sai Organization
- Shirdi Sai Baba – Hindi Literature
- Shirdi Sai Jalaram Mandir
- Shri Saibaba Sansthan, Shirdi
- Sri Gurucharitra
- Sri Sai Baba of Shirdi
- Sri Shirdi Sai Baba Temple

- The Sai Baba of Shirdi
- The Shirdi Sai Avatar
- http://www.saibaba.website.org
- http://www.saibaba.org
- http://www.admn@saibaba.org
- http://www.saijanmasthan.com
- http://www.floridashirdisai.org
- http://www.saidarbarusa.org
- http://www.saimukthi.com
- http://www.saipatham.com
- http://www.saibaba.org
- http://www.shirdisaitemple.com
- http://www.saileela.org
- http://www.saisamadhi.org
- http://www.saimandir.org
- http://www.shirdi.org
- http://www.shirdisaibaba.com
- http://www.templeofpeace.org
- http://www.srisaimarggam.org
- http://www.theshirdisaimandir.com
- http://www.shrishirdisaicanada.org
- http://www.shirdisainath.org
- http://www.saisamsthanusa.org
- http://www.baba.org
- http://www.saibaba.us

Bibliography on Sri Shirdi Sai Baba

1. Agaskar, P.S., *Sri Sai Leelamrita*. Shirdi: Shri Sai Baba Sansthan, 1989. (In Hindi).
2. Aiyer, P.S.V., *Perfect Masters*. Calcutta: Author, 1973.
3. Ajgaonkar, Chakor, *The Divine Glory Sri Shirdi Sai Baba*. New Delhi: Diamond Pocket Books, 1998, pp. 126. (Ed. S.P. Ruhela).
4. _____, *Tales From Sai Baba's Life*. New Delhi: Diamond Pocket Books, 1998, pp. 183 (Ed. S.P. Ruhela)
5. _____, *What Saints & Maters Say on the Realm of Sadhna*. New Delhi: Diamond Pocket Books, 1998, pp. 88 (Ed. S.P. Ruhela)
6. _____, *Foot Prints of Shirdi Sai*. New Delhi: Diamond Pocket Books, 1998. (Ed. S.P. Ruhela)
7. _____, *Sri Shirdi Sai Baba Ki Divya Jeevan Kahani*. New Delhi: Diamond Pocket Books, 1998, pp. 164. (Trans. J.P. Srivastava; Ed. S.P. Ruhela). (In Hindi)
8. _____, *Sri Sai Geetayan*. New Delhi: Diamond Pocket Books, 1998, pp. 93, (Trans. J.P. Srivastava, (Ed. S.P. Ruhela): (In Hindi).
9. Anand, Sai Sharan, *Sri Sai Baba*. Bombay: Dinpushpa Prakashan, 1989. (In Marathi/Gujarati).
10. _____, *Sri Sai Baba*. New Delhi: Sterling Publishers, 1997. (Trans. V.B. Kher) (In English)
11. _____, *Sai; The Supeman*. Shirdi: Shri Sai Baba Sansthan, 1991.
12. _____, Awasthi, Dinesh & Blitz Team of Investigators, "Sai Baba The Saint of Shirdi", *Blitz* (Bombay Weekly), Nov. 6 & 13, 1976. (Article)
13. Balakrishna, V.V., Sri *Sayee Smaromstroram*.
14. Balse, Mayah, *Mystics and Men of Miracles in India*. New Delhi: Orient Paper backs, 1978.
15. Bharadawaja, Acharya, E., *Sai Baba The Master*. Ongole: Sri Guru Paduka Publications, 1991. (III Ed.)

16. Bharati, Sushil, *Sai Darshan Sagar*: Sai Prakashan, 1995, p. 62, (In Hindi).

17. _____, *Sai Upasana*. Sagar, Sai Prakashan, 1995, pp. 36, (In Hindi).

18. _____, *Sai Kripa Ke Pawan Kshan*. Sagar: Sai Prakashan, 1995. (in Hindi).

19. _____, *Sai Dham*. Sagar: Sai Prakashan, 1996. (In Hindi).

20. _____, *Sai Sukh Chalisa*, Sagar, Sai Prakasthan.

21. _____, *Sai Sandesh*. Sagar: Sai Prakashan.

22. _____, *Sai Mahima*. Sagar: Sai Prakashan.

23. _____, *Bachchon Ke Sai*. Sagar: Sai Prakashan.

24. _____, *Sai Geetmala*. Sagar: Sai Prakashan.

25. _____, *Sai Chintan*. New Delhi: Diamond Pocket Books, 1998, pp. 110.

26. _____, *Sai Sri Ke Adbhut Devdoota*. New Delhi: Diamond Pocket Books, 1998, pp. 216.

27. _____, *Sai Kripa Ke Pavan Kshan*. New Delhi: Diamond Pocket Books, 1998, pp. 126.

28. _____, *Sai Sarita*. New Delhi: Diamond Pocket Books, 1998, 1998, pp. 227.

29. Bharucha, Perin S., *Sai Baba of Shirdi*. Shirdi: Shri Sai Baba Sansthan, 1980.

30. Bharvani, A.D. & Malhotra, V., *Shirdi Sri Baba and Sathya Sai Baba are One and Same*. Bombay: Sai Sahitya Samiti, 1983.

31. Bhisma, K.J., *Sadguru Sai Nath Sagunopasama*. Shirdi: Shri Sai Baba Sansthan, 1986. (Marathi).

32. Chatturvedi, B.K. Sai Baba of Shirdi. New Delhi: Diamond Pocket Books, 1998. (Revised Ed. S.P. Ruhela).

33. Chopra, Parveen, 'Shirdi Sai Baba: Beacon of Hope', *Life Positive* (Monthly), New Delhi; Magus Pvt. Ltd. S-487, Greater Kailash, Part I, Jan. 1998, pp. 16-21 (Article).

34. Das, M. Machinder, *Sai-The God on Earth*.

35. Ganu, Das, *Shri SaiNath Stavan Manjari*. Shirdi: Shri Sai Baba Sansthan, (English Trans. Zarine Taraporewala, Bombay: Sai Dhun Enterprises, 1987).

36. _____, *Sai Harkathas*. Madras: All India Sai Samaj, Mylapore.

37. *Gems of Wisdom*, Nagpur: Sri Publicatins.

38. *Guide to Holy Shirdi*. Shirdi: Shri Sai Baba Sansthan.

39. Gunaji, N., Shri Sai Satcharita, Shirdi: Sai Baba Sansthan, 1944.

40. Harper, Marvin Henry, 'The Fakir: Sri Sai Baba of Shirdi' in *Gurus, Swamis, and Avataras: Spiritual Masters and Their American Disciplines.* Philadelphia: Westminister Press, 1972. (Article).

41. Hattingatti, Shaila, *Sai's Story.* Bombay: India Book House, 1991.

42. Hemadpant, *Shri Sai Satcharita*, Shirdi: Shri Sai Baba Sansthan, (In Marathi, Hindi, Gujarati, Telugu, etc.)

43. *Is Sai Baba Living and Helping Now?* Madras: All India Sai Samaj. Mylapore.

44. Jha, Radhanandan *Sai Baba: Sab Ka Malik Ek Hai.* Patna, Sri Sai Baba Trust, 1997, pp. 65. (In Hindi).

45. Joshi, H.S., *Origin and Development of Dattatreya Worship in India.* Baroda: M.S. University of Baroda, 1965. (Chapter 12).

46. Kakade, R.C. & Veerbhadra. A., *Shirdi to Puttaparthi.* Hyderabad: Ira Prakastha, 1989. (In English & Hindi).

47. Kamath, M.V. & Kher, V.B., *Sai Baba of Shirdi: A Unique Saint.* Bombay: Jaico Publishing House, 1991.

48. Karunanada, Swami, *The Uniqueness of the Significance of Sri Sai Baba.* Panvel: Sri Bhagwati Sai Sansthan.

49. Kevin, Shephered, R, D., *Gurus Discovered* (Biographies of Sai Baba & Upasani Maharaj) Cambridge: Anthropoprahia Publicatiuon 1984.

50. Khaparde, G., *Sources of Sai History.* Bangalore: Jupiter Press, 1956.

51. _____, *Shirdi Diary.* Shirdi: Shri Sai Baba Sansthan.

52. Krishna, Indira Anantha, Sai Baba of Shirdi. (Adarsh Chitra Katha-Pictorial).

53. Krishna, S. Gopala K., *Understanding Shirdi Sai.* Hyderabad: Shirdi Sai Mandiram, Chikkadpalli, 1997, pp. 227.

54. Kumar, Anil, *Doctor of Doctors Sri Sai Baba.* Nagpur: Sri Sai Clinic.

55. Kumar: Sudhir, *Shirdi Ke Sai Baba: Chalisa aur Bhajan.* New Delhi: Author, (In Hindi).

56. Maneey, S., *The Eternal Sai.* New Delhi: Diamond Pocket Books, 1997.

57. Mani, Amma B., *Sai Leela Taranagini.* (Parts 1 & 2). Guntur: Authoress.

58. Mehta, Rao Bahadur Harshad B., *The Spiritual Symphony of Shree Sainath of Shirdi.* Baroda: Rana & Patel Press. 1952.

59. Mehta, Vikas, *Hridaya Ke Swami Shri Sai Baba*. New Delhi: Siddartha Publicatins, 10 DSIDC, Scheme 11. Okhla Industrial Area Part 11, 1995. (In Hindi).

60. _____, *Karunamaya Shri Sai Baba*. New Delhi: Siddartha Publications, 1996. (In Hindi).

61. Mittal, N., *World Famous Modern Gurus and Guru Cults*. New Delhi: Family Books, F 2/16, Darya Ganj.

62. Monayan, S.V.G.S., *Sai the Mother and Ansuya, the Amma*. Masulipattanm, Sai Ma Gurudatta Publications, 18/286, Ambani Agraham.

63. Munsiff, Abdul Ghani, "Hazrat Sai Baba", *The Mehar Baba Journal* (Ahmednagar): Vol. 1 1938-39 (Article.)

64. Murthy, G.S., *Understanding Shirdi Sai Baba*. Hyderabad: Sri Shirdi Sai Prema Mandiram, 1977.

65. Narasimhaswamy ji, *Who is Sai Baba of Shirdi?* Madras: All India Sai Samaj, 1980.

66. _____, *Sri Sai Vachnamrita*. Madras: All India Sai Samaj.

67. _____, *Sai Baba's Charters, and Sayings*. Madras: All India Sai Samaj, 1980.

68. _____, *Devotees' Experiences of Sai Baba*. Madras: All India Sai Samaj, 1965. Hyderabad: 1989.

69. _____, *Glimpses of Sai Baba*. Madras: All India Sai Samaj.

70. _____, *Life of Sai Baba*. Madras: All India Sai Samaj.

71. Narayan, B.K., *Saint Shah Waris Ali and Sai Baba*. New Delhi Vikas Publishing House, 1995, pp. 112.

72. Narayanan, C.R., *A Century of Poems on Sri Sai Baba of Shirdi*. Madras: Author, 1994 (11 Ed.)

73. Nimbalkar, M.B., *Sri Sai Satya Charitra*. Poona: Author, 1993 (In Marathi).

74. 108 Names of Sri Shirdi Sai Baba. New Delhi: Sterling Publishers, 1997. Pp. 108. (Pocket Book).

75. Osburne, Arthur. *The Incredible Sai Baba*. Delhi: Orient Longmans, 1970.

76. Paranjape, Makarand, 'Journey to Sai Baba', *Life Positive*, New Delhi: Magus Media Pvt. Ltd. Jan. 1998, pp. 22-23 (Article).

77. Parchure, D.D., *Children's Sai Baba*, Shirdi: Shri Sai Baba Sansthan, 1983. (In English, Hindi)

78. Parchure, S.D., *Shree Sai Mahimashstra*. Bombay: Tardeo Book Depot, 1990.
79. Parthsarthi, R., *Gold Who Walked on Earth*. New Delhi: Sterling Publishers, 1996.
80. _____, *Apostle of Love: Saint Saipadananda*, New Delhi: Sterling Publishers, 1997.
81. *Pictorial Sai Baba*. Shirdi: Sai Baba Sansthan, 1968.
82. Pradhan, M.V., Sri *Sai Baba of Shirdi*: Shirdi Sri Sai Baba Sansthan, 1973.
83. Ramalingaswami, *The Golden Words of Shri Sai Baba*. Shirdi, 1983.
84. _____, *Ambrosia in Shirdi*. Shirdi: Shri Sai Baba Sansthan, 1984.
85. Ramakrishna, K.K., *Sai Baba The Perfect Master*. Pune: Meher Era Publications, Avatar Meher Baba Poona Centre, 441/1, Somwarpeth, 1991.
86. Rao. A.S., *Life History of Shirdi Sai Baba*. New Delhi: Sterling Publishers, 1997, pp. 228 (Eng. Trans. Thota Bhaskar Rao).
87. Rao, A.S., *In Search of the Truth*, New Delhi: Sterling Publishing, 1998.
88. Rao, B. Umamaheswara, Thus Spoke Sri Shirdi Sai Baba. New Delhi: Diamond Pocket Books, 1997. (Ed. S.P. Ruhela)
89. Rao, B. Umamaheswara, *Communications From the Spirit of Shri Shirdi Sai Baba*. New Delhi: Diamond Pocket Books, 1998, pp. 160 (Ed. S.P. Ruhela).
90. _____, *The Spiritual Philosophy of Sri Shirdi Sai Baba*. New Delhi: Diamond Pocket Books, 1998. (Revised edition of *Bhava Lahari: Voice of Sri Sai Baba,* 1993) Ed. S.P. Ruhela.
91. _____, *Sai Leela Tarangini*. Guntur: Author, Flat 12, 'Sai Towers', 4th Line, Brindavan Gardens, Guntur-522006). (In Telugu).
92. _____, *Sai Tatwa Sandesham* (Part I & II). Guntur: Author, (In Telugu).
93. _____, *Sai Tatwa Sandesham*. Guntur: Author. (In English)
94. Rao, evata Sabhe, *Baba Sai*. Hyderabad: 76, N.H.I., Type Ramchandrapuram.
95. Rao, M.S., *Divine Life Story of Sri Sudguru Krishnaprlyaji*. Burla: Author, 1995.
96. Rao, Devata Sabha, *Baba Sai* Hyderabad: 76 N.H.I., Type 5, Ramchandrapuram (BHEL).

97. Rao, K.V. Raghva, *Message of Sri Sai Baba*. Madras: All India Sai Samaj, 1984. (Ed. By Dwarkamai Trust, Hyderabad, 1995).

98. _____, *Message of Shri Sai Baba*. Hyderabad: Shri Shirdi Publications Trust, 1992

99. _____. *Enlightenment From Sri Baba on Salvation of Soul*. Hyderabad: Dwarkamai Publications, 1994.

100. _____. *Golden Voice and Divine Touch of Sri Sai Baba*. Hyderabad: Dwarkamai Publications, 1997.

101. Rao, M. Rajeswara, *Shri Shirdi Sai Baba and His Teaching*. New Delhi: Diamond Pocket Books, 1998, pp. 76 (Ed. S.P. Ruhela) (Mini Book).

102. Rigopoulos, Antonio, *The Life and Teachings of Sri Sai Baba of Shirdi* (Ph. D. Thesis) New York: State University, 1992. (Delhi—110007): Sri Sadguru Publications, Indian Book Centre 40/5, Shakti Nagar 1995).

103. Ruhela, Sushila Devi, *Sri Shirdi Sai Bhajan Sangraha (Samprna)*. New Delhi: Diamond Pocket Books, 1998, pp. 287. (In Hindi)

104. —, *Sri Shirdi Sai Bhajan Sangraha*. New Delhi: Diamond Pocket Books, 1998. Pp. 96.

105. —, *Sri Shirdi Sai Bhajanmala*. New Delhi Diamond Pocket Books, 1998, pp. 135. (Mini Book)

106. Ruhela, S.P., My Life with Shirdi Sai Baba—Thrilling Memories of Shivamma Thayee. Faridabad: Sai Age Publications, 1992. (New Delhi-110002: M.D. Publications, 11, Darya Ganj, 1995).

107. ——, *Sri Shirdi Sai Baba Avatar*. Faridabad: Sai Age Publications, 1992.

108. ——, *What Researchers say on Sri Shirdi Sai Baba*. Faridabad: Sai Age Publications, 1994. (II Ed. New Delhi-110002: M.D. Publications, 1995).

109. ——, *Sri Shirdi Sai Baba: The Universal* Master. New Delhi; Sterling Publishers, L-10, Green Park Extension, 1994. (Reprint 1995, 1996).

110. ——, *The Sai Trinity*—Sri Shirdi Sai, Sri Sathya Sai, Sri Prema Sai Incarnations, New Delhi-110014; Vikas Publishing House, 1994.

111. ——, *Sai Puran*, Delhi: Sadhna Pocket Books, 1996.

112. ——, Shirdi Sai Baba Speaks to Yogi Spencer in Vision, New Delhi: Vikas Publishing House, 1998.

113. ——, *Sant Shiromani Sri Shirdi* Sai Baba, New Delhi: Sterling Publishers, 1997.

114. ——, (Ed) *Divine Revelations of a Sai Devotee*. New Delhi: Diamond Pocket Books, 1997, pp. 270.

115. ——, (Ed.) *Sri Shirdi Sai Bhajan-mala*, (In Roman) New Delhi: Diamond Pocket Books, 1998, pp. 111.

116. ——, *Shirdi Sai Baba's Mother and Her Re-incarnation*. New Delhi: Aravali Books International (W-30, Okhla Industrial Area, Phase-II, New Delhi-110020). 1998, pp. 45. (Pocket Books).

117. ——, (Ed.) New Light on Sri Shirdi Sai Baba. New Delhi: Diamond Pocket Books, 1998.

118. ——, (Ed.) *Shirdi Sai Ideal and The Sai World*. New Delhi: Diamond Pocket Books. 1998.

119. (Ed.), *The Immortal Fakir of Shirdi*, New Delhi: Diamond Pocket Books, 1998.

120. ——, My *Life with Sri Shirdi Sai Baba*. (In Japanese).

121. *Sai Amritvani* (By: B.K. Bassi, 1/42, Panchsheel Park, New Delhi An excellent melodious prayer to Sri Shirdi Sai Baba. This very impressive impressive and highly elevasting prayer is mmost attentively listened by countless Sai devotee throughout the world on Thursday—Sai Baba's favorite day. It may be downloaded from: http://groups.yahoo.com/group/mysaiu baba 20

122. *Sadguru Nityananada Bhagavan The Eternal Entity*. Kanhangad Pin Code 671315. Kerala: Swami Nityananda Ashram, 1996 (IIEd.)

123. *Sai Ma Ki Kripavrasti*—Souvenir, Mussorie, Sai Darbar, 2, Garden Reach. Kulri, 1997. (In Hindi)

124. *Sai Sandesh* (Sri Shirdi Sai Messages give to Devotee). (Parts I & II Hyderabad: Sai Prabha Publications (3050697/87. Telugu Academy Lane, Vithalwadi)

125. Seshadri, H., *Glimpses of Divinity—A Profile of Shri Saidas Babaji*, Bombay: Shri Bhopal Singh Hingharh. (It shows that Sri Shirdi Sai Baba and Sri Sathya Sai Baba are one and the same.)

126. *Sai Sudha*. Magazine—Golden Jubilee Issue, Special Number, Madras: All India Sai Samaj.

127. Savitri, Raghnath, *Sai Bhajanmlal*. Mumbai: Balaji Bagya, Sudarshan Art Printing Press, 5 Vadla Udhyog Bhavan, Mumbai-400031, 1995 (24th Ed. 1986) (In Marathi). (It contains folk songs and Bhajans on Sri Shirdi Sai since his lifetime.)

128. Shepherd, R.D. *Gurus Rediscovered.* Cambridge: Anthropological Publications, 1985. Biographies of Sri Shirdi Sai Baba and Sri Upasani Maharaj).

129. *Shirdi Darshan,* Shirdi, Shri Sai Baba Sansthan, 1966, 1972. (Pictorial).

130. Shirdi Ke Sai Baba. Delhi: Ratna Book Co. (In Hindi)

131. Shivnesh Swamiji, *Sri Sai Bavani,* Shirdi.

132. *Shree Sai Leela: Sachitra Jeevandarshan.* 1939.

133. *Shree Sai Leela,* March—April 1992. (First Convention of Sai Devotees).

134. *Silver Jubilee Souvenir.* Madras: All India Sai Samaj, 1996.

135. *Spiritual Recipes,* Bangalore: Sri Sai Baba Spiritual Centre, Sri Sai Baba Mandir Marg, T. Nagar.

136. Singh. I.D, *Gagar Main Sai Kshir Sagar.* Faridabad; Sai Age Publications, 1996. (In Hindi). (New Delhi: Diamond Pocket Books, 1997)

137. Somsundaram, A., The *Dawn of a New Era: The Message of Master Ram Ram And the Need for Universal Religion.* Markapur (A.P.): Divine Centre, 1970.

138. Somsundaran, A., *The Dawn of New Era: The Vision of Master Rishi Ram Ram.* Markapur: Divine Centre, 1969.

139. *Souvenir: Maha Samadhi Souvenir.* Madras: All India Sai Samaj, 1966.

140. *Souvenir,* Delhi: Shri Sai Bhakta Samaj, 1972.

141. *Souvenir.* Secunderabad: Sri Sai Baba Samaj, 1975.

142. *Souvenir:* Secunderabad: Sri Sai Baba Samaj, 1990.

143. *Souvenir:* 26th All India Sai Devotees Convention: Golden Jubilee Year, 1991.

144. *Sri Harikatha—Special Number on Shirdi Ke Sai Baba.* New Delhi: Srikath, B-5/73, Azad Apartments, Sri Aurobindo Marg (Bilingual).

145. Sri *Sainath Mananan.* (Sanskrit with English). A Symposium: All India Sai Samaj, Mylapore.

146. *Sri Sai Spiritual Centre and The Trinity* (Sai Baba, Sri Narasimha Swamiji, Sri Radhakrishna Swamiji). Bangalore: Sri Sai Spiritual Centre, Sai Baba Mandir Road, Ist Block, Thyagraja Nagar, Bangalore-560028), pp. 36.

147. Steel, Brian, *Sathya Sai Baba Compendium.* York Beach (USA): Samuel Weisner, 1997. Pp. 244-248.

148. Subramaniam, C.S., *The Life and Teachings of Great Sai Baba.*

149. *Tales of Sai Baba.* Bombay: India Book House, 1995. (Pictorial)

150. Tanavde, S.V. May Sai Baba Bless Us All. Bombay: Taradeo Book Depot.

151. Taraporewala, Zarine, *Worship of Manifested Sri Sadguru Sainath.* (English translation of K. J. Bhismas Sri Sadguri Sainath Sahunopasan). Bombay: Saidhun Enterprses 1990.

152. Towards *Godhood*—Messages *Reveived by Autowriting at the Centre* (Third Annual Number). Coimbatore: The Spiritual Healing Centre, 1945. Pp. 6-8 (It contains some Spirit Message on and from Sai Baba received in 1940).

153. Uban, Sujan Singh, 'Sai Baba of Shirdi', *The Gurus of India.* London: 1977.

154. *Verma, Subha, "Shirdi, Sab Boom Sai Ki . . ." Saptahik* Hindustan, Nov. 12, 1992, pp. 17-25. (In Hindi). (Article).

155. Verma, Subha, *Sri Das Ganukrita Char Adhyaya.* New Delhi: Ansh Media Expression. Subha Verma, A-35, Chittaranjan Park, New Delhi-110019), 1997, pp. 46.

156. White, Charles, S. J., 'The Sai Baba Movement: Approaches to the Study of India, Saints', *The Journal of Asian Studies*, Vol. XXXI, (Article) No. 4, August 1972.

Om Sai Namo Namaha,
Shree Sai Namo Namaha,

Jai Jai Sai Namo Namaha,
Sat Guru Sai Namo Nam

****

108 Divine Names
of Sri Shirdi Sai Baba

(*Om* is the name of God)

1. *Om Shri Sainathaya namah.*
(*Om* obeisance to Shri Sai Nath)
2. *Om Shri Sai Lakshminarayanays namah.*
(*Om* obeisance to Shri Sai Nath who is Narayana, Consort of Goddess Lakshmi)
3. *Om Shri Sai Krishna-Rama-Shiva-Maruityadirupaya Namah.*
(*Om* obeisance to Shri Sai Nath, the manifestation of Lord Krishna, Ram, Shiva, Maruti & others)
4. *Om Shri Sai Shes-shayine Namah.*
(*Om* obeisance to Shri Sai Nath, the Manifestation of Lord Vishnu resting on the thousand headed snake)
5. *Om Shri Sai Godavri-tata-sidhi-vasnih namah.*
(*Om* obeisance to Shri Nath, who made Shirdi on the banks of river Godavari his abode)
6. *m Shri Sai Bhakta-hridalayaya Namah.* (*Om*, obeisance to Shri Sai Nath who dwell in his devotees hearts)
7. *Om Shri Sai Sarva-hrinnilayaya Namah.*
(*Om* obeisance to Shri Sai Nath who dwells in the hearts of all beings)
8. *Om Shri Sai Bhuta-vasaya namah.*
(*Om* obeisance to Shri Sai Nath who is in the hearts of all living creatures)
9. *Om Shri Sai Bhuta-Vhavishyad-bhava varjitaya namah.*
(*Om* obeisance to Shri Sai Nath who does not allow the thoughts of past and future to torment the mind)
10. *Om Shri Sai Kata-teetaya namah.*
(*Om* obeisance to Sri Sai Nath who is beyond the limitations of time)

11. *Om Shri Sai Kataya namah.*
    (*Om* obeisance to Shri Sai Nath who is time incarnate)
12. *Om Shri Sai kalkalaya namah.*
    (*Om* obeisance to Shri Sai Nath who is the Lord of eternity)
13. *Om Shri Sai Kal-darpa-damanaya namah.*
    (*Om* obeisance to Shri Sai Nath, who has destroyed the pride of death)
14. *Om Shri Sai Mrtyunjayaya namaha.*
    (*Om* obeisance to Shri Sai Nath who has conquered death)
15. *Om Shri Sai Amartyaya namah.*
    (*Om* obeisance to Shri Sai Nath who is immortal)
16. *Om Shri Sai Martyabhaya-pradaya namah.*
    (*Om* obeisance to Shri Sai Nath who grants freedom from the fear of death)
17. *Om Shri Sai Jivadharaya namah.*
    (*Om* obeisance to Shri Sai Nath who is the support of all living beings)
18. *Om Shri Sai sarydharyaya namah.*
    (*Om* obeisance to Shri Sai Nath who is the support of the Universe)
19. *Om Shri Sai Bhaktavana-samarthaya namah.*
    (*Om*obeisance to Shri Sai Nath who grants power to his devotees)
20. *Om Shri Sai Bhaktavana-pratigyaya namah.*
    (*Om* obeisance to Shri SaiNath who has vowed to protect his devotees)
21. *Om Shri Sai Anna-Vastra daya namah.*
    (*Om* obeisance to Shri Sai Nath, the bestower of good health and freedom from diseases)
22. *Om Shri Sai Dhana-mangalya-pradaya namah.*
    (*Om* obeisance to Shri Sai Nath, who grants wealth and happiness)
23. *Om Shri Sai Riddhi-Siddhi-daya namah.*
    (*Om* obeisance to Shri Sai Nath who bestows psychic and spiritual powers).
24. *Om Shri Sai Putra-mitra-kalatrabandhu-daya namah.*
    (*Om,* obeisance to Shri Sai Nath who grants sons, friends, spouse and relatives)
25. *Om Shri Sai Yoga-kshaema-vahya namah.*
    (*Om* Obeisance to Shri Sai Nath who undertakes the responsibility of providing for and sustaining the devotees)

26. *Om Shri Sai Apad-bandhavaya namah.*
    (*Om* obeisance to Shri Sai Nath who protects his devotees like friends)
27. *Om Shri Sai Marga-bandhava namah.*
    (*Om* obeisance to Shri Sai Nath who is a companion on life's path)
28. *Om Shri Sai Bhukti-mukti-svargapavarga-daya namah.*
    (*Om* obeisance to Shri Sai Nath who is the bestower of worldly pleasure, salvation, heavenly bliss and ultimate beatitude)
29. *Om Shri Sai Priyaya namah.*
    (*Om* Obeisance to Shri Sai Nath, the beloved)
30. *Om Shri Sai Priti-vardhanaya namah.*
    (*Om* obeisance to Shri Sai Nath who provides capacity for boundless love)
31. *Om Shri Sai Antaryamine namah.*
    (*Om* Obeisance to Shri Sai Nath who is familiar with the innermost secrets of heart)
32. *Om Shri Sai Sahhidatmane namah.*
    (*Om* obeisance to Shri Sai Nath who is symbol of truth and pure consciousness)
33. *Om Shri Sai Nityanandya namah.*
    (*Om* obeisance to Shri Sai Nath who is the embodiment of eternal bliss)
34. *Om Shri Sai Parama-sukha-daya namah.*
    (*Om* obeisance to Shri Sai Nath who bestows supreme happiness)
35. *Om Shri Sai Parmeshwaraya namah.*
    (*Om* obeisance to Shri Sai Nath, the Supreme Lord)
36. *Om Shri Sai Bhakti-Shakti-Pradaya namah.*
    (*Om* obeisance to Shri Sai Nath who grants strength for devotion)
37. *Om Shri Sai Gyana-vairagya-daya namah.*
    (*Om* obeisance to Shri Sai Nath who is the bestower of knowledge and freedom from worldly desires)
38. *Om Shri Sai Prema-Pradaya namah.*
    (*Om* obeisance to Shri Sai Nath, who grants love)
39. *Om Shri Sai Sanshaya hirdaya-daurbalyapapa-karma-vasana kshaya namah.*
    (*Om,* obeisance to Shri Sai Nath who removes doubts, human weakness and inclination to sinful deeds and desire)
40. *Om Shri Sai Hridaya-granthi-bhedkaya namah.*
    (*Om* obeisance to Shri Sai Nath who unbinds all the knots in the heart)

41. *Om Shri Sai karma-dhvansine namah.*
    (*Om* obeisance to Shri Sai Nath who destroys the effects of past evil deeds)
42. *Om Shri Sai Shuddha-sattvasthitaya namah.*
    (*Om* obeisance to Shri Sai Nath who inspires pure and pious thoughts)
43. *Om Shri Sai Gunatita-gunatmane namah.*
    (*Om* obeisance to Shri Sai Nath who attributes is endowed with all wirtues and yet transcends them all)
44. *Om Shri Sai Ananta-kalyana-gunaya namah.*
    (*Om* obeisance to Shri Sai Nath who has limitless virtuous attributes)
45. *Om Shri Sai Amita-parakramaya namah.*
    (*Om* obeisance to Shri Sai Nath who has unlimited Supreme power)
46. *Om Shri Sai Jayine namah.*
    (*Om* obeisance to Shri Sai Nath, who is the personification of victory)
47. *Om Shri Sai Durdharshakshobhyaya namah.*
    (*Om* obeisance to Shri Sai Nath who is unchallengeable and impossible to defy)
48. *Om Shri Sai Aparajitaya namah.*
    (*Om* obeisance to Shri Sai Nath who is unconquerable)
49. *Om Shri Sai Trilokeshu Avighata-gataye namah.*
    (*Om,* obeisance to Shri Sainath, the Lord of three worlds whose actions there are no obstructions)
50. *Om Shri Sai Ashakya-rahitaya namah.*
    (*Om* obeisance to Shri Sai Nath for whom nothing is impossible)
51. *Om Shri Sai Sarva-Shakti-Murtaye namah.*
    (*Om* obeisance to Shri Sai Nath, who is the Almightly, the Omnipotent)
52. *Om Shri Sai Suroopa-sundaraya namah.*
    (*Om* obeisance to Shri Sai Nath who has a beautiful form)
53. *Om Shri Sai Sulochanaya namah.*
    (*Om* obeisance to Shri Sai Nath whose eyes are beautiful and whose glance is auspicious)
54. *Om Shri Sai Bahurupa-vishva-murtaye namah.*
    (*Om* obeisance to Shri Sai Nath who is of various form, and is manifest in the form of Universe itself)
55. *Om Shri Sai Arupavyakatya namah.*
    (*Om* obeisance to Shri Sai Nath who is formless and whose image cannot be bound in mere word)

56. *Om Shri Sai Achintaya namah.*
(*Om* obeisance to Shri Sai Nath who is inconceivable and incomprehensible)

57. *Om Shri Sai Sookshmaya namah.*
(*Om* obeisance to Shri Sai Nath who dwells within every minute creature)

58. *Om Shri Sai Sarvantaryamine namah.*
(*Om* obeisance to Shri Sai Nath who dwells in all souls)

59. *Om Shri Sai Manovagatitaya namah.*
(*Om* obeisance to Shri Sai Nath who is the familiar with the thoughts, speech and past of the devotees)

60. *Om Shri Sai Prema-murtaye namah.*
(*Om* obeisance to Shri Sai Nath who is the embodiment of love and affection)

61. *Om Shri Sai Sulabha-durlabhaya namah.*
(*Om* obeisance to Shri Sai Nath who is easily accessible to his devotes but inaccessible to the wicked)

62. *Om Shri Sai Asahaya-sahayaya namah.*
(*Om* obeisance to Shri Sai Nath who is the supporter of the helpless)

63. *Om Shri Sai Anathanatha-decna-bandhave namah.*
(*Om* obeisance to Shri Sai Nath who is the protector of the unprotected and the kinsman of the destitute)

64. *Om Shri Sai Sarva-bhara-bhric namah.*
(*Om* obeisance to Shri Sai Nath who takes over entire burden of all)

65. *Om Shri Sai Akannaneka-karma-sukannine namah.*
(*Om* obeisance to Shri Sai Nath who himself is the non-doer yet inspires others to perform numberless virtuous deeds)

66. *Om Shri Sai Punya-shravana-keertanaya namah.*
(*Om* obeisance to Shri Sai Nath hearing about whom and speaking of whose glories, is an act of religious merit)

67. *Om Shri Sai Tirthaya namah.*
(*Om* obeisance to Shri Sai Nath who is the embodiment of all holy places)

68. *Om Shri Sai Vasudevaya namah.*
(*Om* obeisance to Shri Sai Nath who is the incarnation of Lord Krishna i.e. Vasudeva)

69. *Om Shri Sai Satam gataya namah.*
(*Om* obeisance to Shri Sai Nath who guides the devotees on the noble and cirtuous path)

70. *Om Shri Sai Sat-parayanaya namah.*
    (*Om* obeisance to Shri Sai Nath, who is fully dedicated to truth)
71. *Om Shri Sai Loknathaya namah.*
    (*Om* obeisance to Shri Sai Nath who is the Lord of the Universe)
72. *Om Shri Sai Pavananghayanamah.*
    (*Om* obeisance to Shri Sai Nath whuo is pure and free form sins)
73. *Om Shri Sai Amritanshave namah.*
    (*Om* obeisance to Shri Sai Nath who is ambrosial)
74. *Om Shri Sai Bhaskara-prabhaya namah.*
    (*Om*obeisance to Shri Sai Nath who is lustrous like the sun)
75. *Om Shri Sai Brahmacharya-tapashcharyadi-suvrataya namah.*
    (*Om* obeisance to Shri Sai Nath who has adopted celibacy, sceticism, devout austerity and other spiritual disciplines)
76. *Om Shri Sai Sathya-dharma-parayanaya namah.*
    (*Om* obeisance to Shri Sai Nath who has taken to truth and righteousness)
77. *Om Shri Sai Siddhesvaraya namah.*
    (*Om* obeisance toi Shri Sai Nath who is the incarnation of Shiva i.e. Siddheswar)
78. *Om Shri Sai Siddha-sankalpaya namah.*
    (*Om* obeisance to Shri Sai Nath whose determination prevails)
79. *Om Shri Sai Yogeshvaraya namah.*
    (*Om* obeisance to Shri Sai Nath who is Yogeshwar i.e. incarnation of Lord Shiva & Lord Krishna)
80. *Om Shri Sai Bhagavati namah.*
    (*Om* obeisance to Shri Sai Nath who is the Divinity)
81. *Om Shri Sai Bhakta-vatsalaya namah.*
    (*Om* obeisance to Shri Sai Nath who is full of love for his devotees)
82. *Om Shri Sai Satpurushaya namah.*
    (*Om* obeisance to Shri Sai Nath the virtuouos, pious & venerable one)
83. *Om Shri Sai Purushottamaya namah.*
    (*Om* obeisance to Shri Sai Nath who is the incarnation of the Supreme i.e. Lord Rama)
84. *Om Shri Sai Sathya-tattva-bodhakaya namah.*
    (*Om* obeisance to Shri Sai Nath who is the preceptor of the essence of truth)

85. *Om Shri Sai Kamadi-sad-vair-dhvansine namah.*
    (*Om* obeisance to Shri Sai Nath who destroys all worldly desires i.e. lust, nager, greed, delusion, ego and envy)
86. *Om Shri Sai Abhed-anand-anubhav-pradaya namah.*
    (*Om,* obeisance to Shri Sai Nath to the bestower of the bliss arising from oneness with God)
87. *Om Shri Sai Sama-Sarva-mata-sammmataya namah.*
    (*Om,* obeisance to Shri Sai Nath who preaches that all religions are equal)
88. *Om Shri Sai Dakshina-murtayenamah.*
    (*Om* obeisance to Shri Sai Nath who is himself Lord Dakshinamurti i.e. Shiva)
89. *Om Shri Sai Venkateshharamanaya namah.*
    (*Om* obeisance to Shri Sai Nath who is remains merged in Lord Venkateshwara i.e. Vishnu)
90. *Om Shri Sai Adbutananta-charyayanamah.*
    (*Om* obeisance to Shri Sai who is Divine and is ever engrossed in blissful meditation)
91. *Om Shri Sai Prapannarti-haraya namah.*
    (*Om* obeisance to Shri Sai Nath who eradicates the distress of those who take refuge in him)
92. *Om Shri Sai Sansara-sarva-duhkha-kshaya-karaya namah.*
    (*Om* obeisance to Shri Sai Nath who destroys all the calamities of the world)
93. *Om Shri Sai Sarvavit-sarvato-mukhaya namah.*
    (*Om* obeisance to Shri Sai Nath who is omniscient and omnipresent)
94. *Om Shri Sai Saravantar-bahih-sthitaya namah.*
    (*Om* obeisance to Shri Sai Nath who exists everywhere and in everything)
95. *Om Shri Sai Sarva-mangala-karaya namahavde.*
    (*Om* obeisance to Shri Sai Nath who is the bestower of auspiciousness)
96. *Om Shri Sai Sarvabhista-pradaya namah.*
    (*Om* obeisance to Shri Sai Nath who established amity and harmony amongst followers of diverse religions leading to a common path of virtue)
97. *Om Shri Sai Samarth Sadguru Sainathaya namahh.*
    (*Om* obeisance to Shri Sai Nath who is the most powerful and the Supreme Guru in Spiritual life).

98. *Om Shri Sai Dakshina-murtayenamah.*
   (Om obeisance to Shri Sai Nath who is himself Lord Dakshinamurti i.e. Shiva)

99. *Om Shri Sai Venkateshharamanaya namah.*e
   (Om, obeisance to Shri Sai Nath who remains merged in Lord Venkateshwara i.e. Vishnu)

100. *Om Shri Sai Adbutananta-charyayanamah.*
   (Om, obeisance to Shri Sai who is Divine and is ever engrossed in blissful meditation)

101. *Om Shri Sai Prapannarti-haraya namah.*
   (Om obeisance to Shri Sai Nath who eradicates the distress of those who take refuge in Him).

102. *Om Shri Sai Sansara-sarva-duhkha-kshaya-karaya namah.*l
   (Om obeisance to Shri Sai Nath who destroys all the calamities of the world)

103. *Om Shri Sai Sarvavit-sarvato-mukhaya namah.*
   (Om obeisance to Shri Sai Nath who is Omniscient and Omnipresent)

104. *Om Shri Sai Saravantar-bahih-sthitaya namah.*ro
   (Om obesiance to Shri Sai Nath who exists everywhere and in everything)

105. *Om Shri Sai Sarva-mangala-karaya namah.*
   (Om obeisance to Shri Sai Nath who is the bestower of auspiciousness)

106. *Om Shri Sai Sarvabhista-pradaya namah.*
   (Om obeisance to Shri Sai Nath who grants all desires)

107. *Om Shri Sai Samarasa-sanmarya-sthapanaya namah.*
   (Om, obeisance to Shri Sai Nath who established amity and harmony amongst followers of diverse religions leading to a common path of virtue).

108. *Om Shri Sai Samarth Sadguru sainathaya namah. and*
   (Om obeisance to Shri Sai Nath who is the most powerful and the Supreme Guru in Spiritual life).

THE END